ANTIQUE DOLLS
OF CHINA & BISQUE

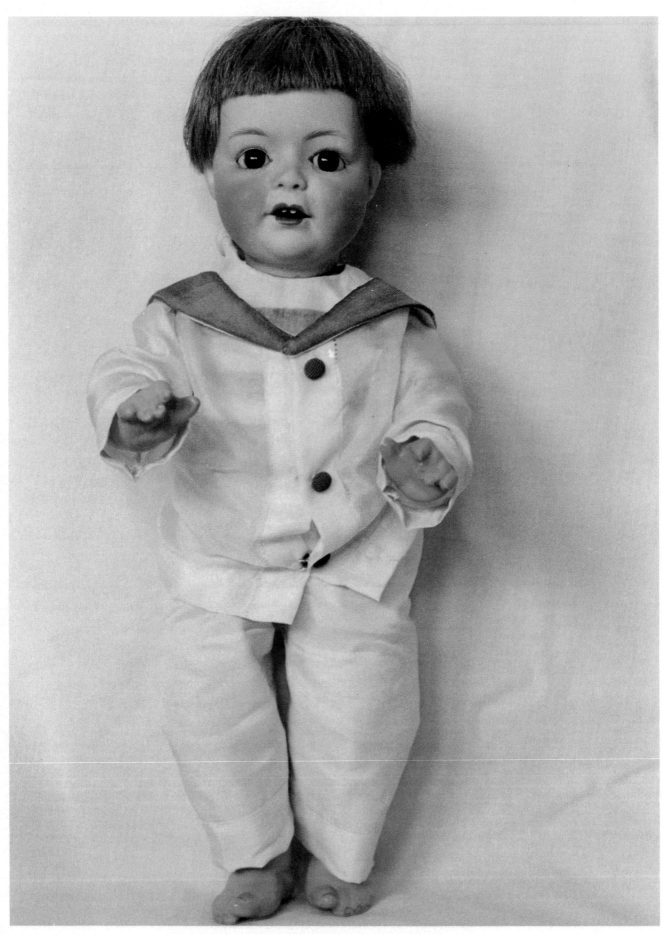

CHARACTER BISQUE HEADED DOLL BY GEBR. HEUBACH, 5H. *Private collection, Queensland*

ANTIQUE DOLLS
OF CHINA & BISQUE

Marjory Fainges

ROBERT HALE • LONDON

Acknowledgments

I wish to thank the following for all their help and support and for allowing me to photograph their dolls so that they may be included in this book.

Betty Belcher, Inge Blessas, Pat Blyth, Dorothy Boland, the late Dorothy Brice, and a very special thanks to Jacki Brooks of the *Australian Doll Digest*, Betty Brown, Doreen Budd, Ceramic Supply Centre Brisbane, Jan Clarke, Irene Coleman, Emily Cook, Donna Gilliland, Dawn Moonie and daughter Juelle of Doll & Toy Collection, "Entally House", Nancy Ferguson, David Gibson, Curator "Newstead House" Brisbane, Lesley Hurford for her marvellous help, Tess Jones and Janet Jones for the help they so freely gave, Shirley McKay, Bess Nicholson, Jill Phillips of Discovery Corner, Angela Donovan, Pam Storer of Granny's, Nanette Theodore and Vera Woodhead and the many kind doll owners who have allowed me to photograph and examine their dolls over the years.

A special thanks also goes to Ted's Photographic store, Brisbane and to the manager and staff of Photo 45, Alderley Brisbane who went out of their way to get many of the photographs just right for publication.

A special thanks to my husband Jim who has done all the artwork and to him and son Keith for putting up with meals at odd hours and a book and paper strewn livingroom while this book was being completed.

Book designed by Linda Maxwell with jacket design by Darian Causby.
Front jacket: Top, left: Gbr. Heubach 9578, centre: Simon & Halbig 1079, right: Bahr & Proschild. *Bottom*, left: Jumeau 1907, right: Heubach Koppelsdorf 321/0.

First published in Great Britain 1992

ISBN-0-7090-4844-0

Robert Hale Limited
Clerkenwell House
Clerkenwell Green
London EC1R 0HT

Printed in Singapore by Global Com Pte Ltd

Contents

Head of unmarked 'Clapper' Jester. When stomach is pressed, hands holding cymbals come together and clap.
Private collection, Brisbane

Introduction

This book is about the dolls that the majority of doll collectors are interested in collecting. Such dolls, because of the industrial revolution in Europe, began their climb to popularity as playthings in the early half of last century to reach the peak of excellence in the later years of the 19th century, and the magnificent character dolls in the early part of the 20th century. Beginning with the manufacture of the simple glazed shoulderplate doll heads which were often made in the porcelain factories of Germany, these dolls, or parts to make them, were sent in large numbers to the Americas, Australia and Europe. Many of these were later refined and produced in unglazed china or bisque. With the advent of bisque which produced a much more delicate and lifelike rendition of a ladylike doll's head, the famous fashion or lady doll evolved. These heads were attached to miniature adultlike bodies and dressed in the fashion of the day and some even had complete wardrobes. These dolls and the beautiful French Bébés of the late 1800s were not the playthings of the ordinary child. They were sent to all corners of the globe to be shown and to win awards at various exhibitions worldwide.

Thus the now much sought after dolls by famous makers like Jumeau, Bru and Simon & Halbig found their way into many homes. These exquisite dolls were to be followed by the more prolific but often equally beautiful manufactured dolls by the large German manufacturers such as Armand Marseille and Kestner. Such products and many others, ranging from excellent quality to the rather poorly painted and simply dressed dolls in cotton chemises (costing only a few pence), found their way into nearly every household where there was a young girl.

This point was brought home to me recently when I saw a photograph (taken at the beginning of this century) of a barefoot girl standing outside a miner's cottage in southern Arizona, U.S.A., clutching her jointed bisque headed doll which was better dressed than she was.

Twelve years of dealing directly with the general public as museum curator and owner of one of the largest private doll museums in Australia, lecturer, researcher and author, as well as identifying dolls at doll shows and so on, has made me realise that collectors everywhere are eager to know more about the dolls in their possession.

Many of the dolls featured in this book are the dolls that I have been constantly asked to identify over the years.

The people seeking more information fall roughly into the following categories.

The person who has been fortunate enough to have a doll or dolls that once belonged to a distant relative and have been passed down through the family, actually becoming a family heirloom. Such a doll is often the nucleus of a doll collection.

The antique or second-hand dealer who has come across some 'old' dolls when buying an estate and doesn't know where to look to find out how to identify what he has in his possession.

The growing number of people who are making reproductions of the beautiful old bisque headed dolls, and who are always looking for information to help them with the doll that they are aiming to represent—such as placement of eyelashes and what clothes the dolls may have worn.

The most important clientele of all—doll collectors—who want to know more about the doll or dolls in their collections. They want to become familiar with other dolls, dolls that they may one day want to buy and add to their collection; dolls that they have only read about, and those that have often been referred to only by a number. They wish to know what such a doll should look like, to be able to tell the difference between a French and a German made doll and become familiar with some of the hints for easy identification.

Caring for Your Doll

Caring for the dolls in your collection is a very important part of being a doll collector. A doll support on a proper stand in a glass fronted cupboard or display cabinet is a very good way of preserving your doll. To put one of the modern metal stands on your doll, take the metal grip part out of the base, place it around the doll's waist (either under or over the doll's clothing—that is a personal preference) and then gently replace the gripping part of the stand into the upright part of the base. If the gripping part is too small it will injure both kid and composition bodies. For this reason many doll collectors prefer to make their own stands for use in their display cabinets. They make or have them made with a shaped wooden base 13 mm (½″) thick for stability, with a 9 mm (⅜″) dowel inserted into the base towards the back. The doll is then tied onto the dowel in several places with ordinary cotton tape.

If the doll is strung with cotton covered rubber (the correct rubber to use) the tension and condition of the rubber should be checked every year. This stops the tragedy of finding the head of the doll (maybe cracked or broken) on the shelf, if the old rubber string should give way. It is also advisable to have each jointed leg strung separately to the head hook, so if one leg's elastic should give way the head is retained (this does not apply to baby type bodies). It is best to string a baby body head to legs, except for those that may have partial cloth bodies. Jointed arms are strung separately across the body from one side to the other. Stringing should never be too tight, as this tends to do a great deal of damage to the sockets and often a leg or arm is drawn inside the body, causing massive damage and necessitating a costly repair job. The doll should be strung firmly enough for her to just stand on her own. If you are in doubt about the stringing of your doll, leave it, place the doll in a much safer position, and consult someone who is competent in this type of repair.

If you have to transport your doll for any reason try to place a softly crunched ball of tissue inside the head to stop damage from the eye weight, making sure you don't dislodge the eyes. Wrap the head in one or two clean disposable nappies—they are ideal as they offer plenty of cushioning. Should your old doll have bisque arms or legs, it is always wise to wrap one in some form of cushioning if you have to transport the doll any distance, as this lessens the likelihood of breakage due to the limbs banging against each other.

No doll should ever be left in a cupboard or cabinet where direct sunlight shines at any time during the day, as this tends to fade the clothing very quickly. Many collectors are unaware that they should also be very careful when installing lighting in their display cupboards, as fluorescent lighting too close to a doll also causes clothing to fade.

Many collectors like to change the often rather tatty hair on an old doll for a more glamorous looking modern wig. If you wish to keep the old wig on the doll, a hat made to suit the doll's period does wonders to disguise the tattiness. If you must replace the wig, keep the old one in acid free tissue (definitely not a plastic bag), label it as to which doll it belongs to, and if you ever wish to sell, the old wig should go with the doll.

Many collectors like to redress their dolls. If the old doll has remnants of what was her old dress, why not copy this style in a suitable material, remembering that nylon in materials or laces was introduced only in the 1950s, so is unsuitable for any doll before that date; it is best to keep to cotton laces on your old dolls. Cottons, taffetas, voiles, velvets and silks are all good for dressing your old bisque headed dolls. Again, if you are redressing, keep the remnants of the doll's old clothing in acid free tissue, not plastic. *No doll, parts of dolls or clothing should ever be kept in plastic.* If you wish to store your doll or dolls away and not have them on display, a well washed pillowcase or old sheeting is ideal.

Researching Your Doll

While there are many excellent books now available on dolls, I have found over the years that many are either very expensive, very selective with overseas trends, or written in general terms that fail to incorporate the required information requested by many doll collectors to help them identify their dolls.

Through the exhaustive work done by doll researchers it is now known that many manufacturers of dolls' heads of bisque china, such as Armand Marseille, Simon & Halbig etc., made heads to order for doll assembly companies in other countries.

Thus these specially designated doll head mould numbers may appear only in one country, or be prolific in one country and rare in another. For example dolls bearing the Kestner trademark and mould numbers are quite common in the United States, but only a few Kestner mould numbers are found on dolls in Australia. The prolific 390 mould number of Armand Marseille, especially in size 7, is very common in Australia, whereas the sizes 6 and 8 are more prevalent in Europe. The Armand Marseille mould numbers 382 and 384-character baby, flange neck doll heads appear to have been sent to Australia only, and in rather limited quantities.

Although numerous books have been written on dolls of all kinds over the last 50 years, many of these books show only the beautiful and rare dolls that are now seen in museums and are out of the financial reach of the average doll collector.

This book caters not only for those who aspire to own a very elusive and expensive doll, but also for the majority of doll collectors for whom there are thousands of ordinary and unusual old and antique dolls that are worth collecting.

The photographs in this book have been taken by me through the kind courtesy and permission of doll collectors (such as those mentioned) and by the auspices of doll dealers who supply their demands.

From the beautiful and elegant French Bébés to the wonderful bisque headed character dolls of the early decades of this century to the mass produced rather poor quality 1930s Japanese dolls, all can be found in the pages of this book, and for easier identification the book has been produced in alphabetical order with cross references.

Preserving the Heritage of Your Doll

Preserving the heritage or 'provenance' of your old doll that has been passed down to you or bought from the original owner is very important. You may do this in two ways. I always suggest that you find out everything you can positively get to know about the doll's history, such as where and when bought, price if known, when it was given and to whom and how it was handed down, and what the doll has been called. Write all this information in indelible pen or pencil onto a piece of washed lawn. This can then be tacked to the inside of the underclothes, such as a petticoat, or on a long piece of lawn that is put around the body and tacked together at the back. Another way is to write or type the information and keep it with the doll, but this tends to get lost, so I prefer the first method. Thus the doll becomes part of your family's history, and it actually gives the doll a little extra value if its history is correctly kept.

Prices etc.

Some doll collectors may be disappointed that this is not a price guide, but please remember, a price guide in book form is often out of date before it is published. Fashions and fads abound in doll collecting and prices are constantly fluctuating from one month to the next. Although this book has no prices you will find it handy for furthering your knowledge, enabling you to identify dolls that interest you at an auction or doll fair. Your best guide to what a doll is worth is to follow current auction prices and check the prices of similar dolls at doll fairs and so on, always remembering that there is a buying and a selling price for every doll and these two prices may differ dramatically depending on who is doing the buying or selling. Dolls on sale at top price must be in top condition to warrant the price asked.

Buying a Doll

When you are buying a doll, always handle it carefully; remember it is not yours till you have paid for it, and if you damage it you are liable. There appears to be a trend at the moment to test the ring of the doll's bisque head with a finger ring to see if it rings true. This should not be done at all, for although it might give you the sound you are looking for, it can also cause damage by chipping the head and causing minute cracks. This is a very bad practice which should not be followed.

Before you buy a doll, ask to have the wig and pate removed; do it nicely, and a genuine doll collector or good dealer will always oblige. Years ago wigs were often glued down tightly on the head to hide cracks and chips out of the back of the head. I have come across this quite a lot when lifting old wigs to repair dolls. Also ask if you can see the doll undressed so that you can check that the head fits in the socket where it should and there is no damage or little damage to the body.

A broken head on a bisque doll drops the price dramatically. A chipped or cracked head lowers the value of the doll as does a replacement body or a badly damaged body. So if you are looking for a cheap doll, you will find you end up either with a cracked head or a modern replacement body; it's up to you, but the modern body does not lower the value as much as a bad crack or bad chip.

Conclusion

Over the last twenty years there has been considerable research into the origin of dolls and so more information has become available, giving us all a better knowledge of the manufacturers of the dolls we all love looking at and collecting. Old ideas of who made what have had to be revised as more information has come to hand, and what was commonly accepted five to fifteen or more years ago (and found in books written in those years or before) may not always agree with what is now known and included in this book. Terminology used in referring to types of dolls may also have changed.

A great deal of sifting through books by such well known writers on dolls as Jan Foulke, Dorothy, Elizabeth Anne and Evelyn Jane Coleman, the Ciesliks, Mary Hillier and the Pollocks, as well as many others in my own vast personal library, has enabled me to bring to you the most up-to-date knowledge that I have been able to find as of the beginning of 1991.

No doubt in the next ten years or so even more knowledge may emerge on these dolls, and hopefully more will be written on the manufacture of Japanese bisque dolls and also on the history of old and antique dolls manufactured in other countries such as Italy. To further your knowledge of dolls read any book on the subject that you can. Many libraries now carry a range of doll related books. Join a doll club and buy doll magazines. All will help you gain more knowledge and enjoy your hobby even more.

I have found that I have learnt a lot more about dolls during my research to identify dolls that have been shown to me, many of which appear in this book; this information has been passed on to you through the many photographs, so that in the future you will be able to say 'so that is what my doll is' while at the same time learning a little about the history of the manufacturer.

After reading this book, I hope all collectors will be proud of the dolls in their own collections, appreciate and enjoy other collections and refrain from the often heard phrase 'It's only a —!' All these dolls, whether of excellent bisque or rather poorly painted, are worthy of collecting.

Flat top china head, exposed ears, red line above eyes. Original clothes.

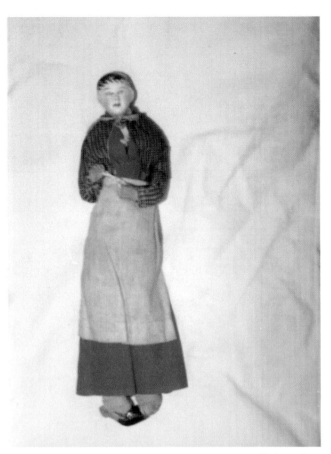

Very short painted hairstyle on a china headed doll dressed in European provincial costume. *Queensland*

Unglazed china head and arms, but hair has been glazed. Original clothes. Simple painting, exposed ears. Although dressed as a woman this doll's head may have been meant to have been that of a man or boy. *Private collection, Brisbane*

Two small 'low brow' dolls, one on left with black hair, one on right blonde. All original clothing, could have once been used in a doll's house. Doll on left is glazed china, doll on right unglazed china. *Private collection, Tasmania*

China Dolls

The china doll industry developed primarily in the Bavarian and Thuringian regions of Germany with the towns of Nuremberg, Coburg and Sonneberg being the main production centres. Unfortunately few of the millions of china dolls' heads were marked, so that even though some of the manufacturers of these dolls are now known, it is very hard to say where each type of head originated and who manufactured it. The other reason is that many doll factories copied each other.

What Is a China Doll?

It is a doll that has a glazed or shiny doll's head that was mainly manufactured in Germany from the early 1800s until the 1920s. Nearly all china dolls' heads were made from a mixture of white kaolin clay, feldspar and silica. The multitudes of these dolls heads were produced by one of two methods.

The main method used before 1880 was that of press moulding. The prepared clay was kneaded, then rolled until it was a thin even paste. This paste was then pressed into the two halves of the head mould. The heads were then placed in large heated rooms where they were left to dry out. When dried to the right consistency, they were assembled, cleaned and fired in huge ovens with up to 5000 heads in one oven at a time.

The second method, popular from around the 1880s until china doll head manufacture ceased, was to pour thinned paste or slip into the complete head mould, leave for an allotted time and pour out the remaining slip, leaving a thin shell of porcelain slip in the mould. These too were left to dry and then fired.

When the blank heads made by both methods had cooled each head was painted—the moulded hair, eyes, mouth and a touch of colour on the cheeks. A feldspathic glaze was then applied and another firing took place. The finished heads had a high glossy finish. The early heads that were pressed into the moulds are uneven on the inside due to the pressing. The later poured heads are smooth, except some have tiny fine bubbles which were incurred when pouring.

Many of the early doll heads have tiny black dots, which were formed from the impurities in the original clay. These tiny black spots, while not found in all early china heads, are an aid to help verify that your china head is not a reproduction.

Some of the dolls of last century were manufactured with fully moulded bald heads with a painted pate. The painted pate was either a finishing mark or designated where to glue the appropriate wig.

Many collectors have incorrectly called bald china headed dolls 'Biedermeier dolls'. These bald headed dolls, depending on wigs and clothing, could represent male or female dolls. Bald headed dolls, especially with painted pates, are generally considered rarer than those with moulded hairstyles.

The majority of dolls' heads with moulded hair are quite formal looking and mainly represent a head of a woman. The hair is moulded as part of the head, and some hairstyles,

Low brow china head, centre part, dressed in original clothes. Red and white material with Kate Greenaway type dressed girls printed around edge of overcape. *Melbourne*

Centre part china head, short curls all around head. *Author's collection*

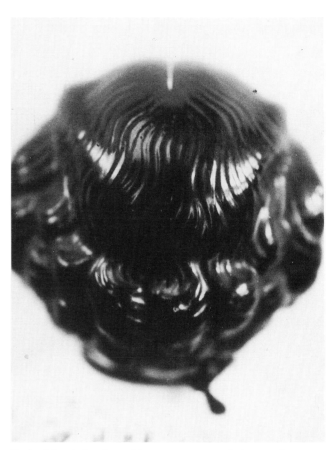

Back of head showing white centre part and short curls.

China headed doll, centre part, hair swept to side, red line above eyes. *Circa* 1830. *Author's collection*

particularly between 1850 and 1880, are quite elaborate. Some of these dolls even have pierced ears so that earrings can complement their hairstyles.

The many variations of hair styles found on china dolls' heads are the main source for determining their age, and they can usually be dated within a twenty year span. It must be remembered though, that there is always the exception as a few hairstyles were so popular that they lasted for decades.

A very general means of hair dating:

1830–1840 Long hair parted in the centre, hair draped below the ears, sometimes swept back into a bun or twist.

1850–1860s Dolls hairstyles are quite elaborate, often having ornamentation, such as bands or moulded snoods as part of their moulded hair. During the years 1840–1860 many centre partings were left white.

1870–1880 A variety of hairstyles too numerous to mention.

1890–1910 Low brow hairdos, with wavy curls that fell low on the forehead.

Nearly all glazed china hairstyles before 1880 were painted black, the not so common blonde, and the very rare brown. After 1880 blonde coloured moulded hair became more prevalent.

The painting of the eyes was simple, blue with a small black spot for the iris. Most of the heads had fine black eyelining and red dots in the corner of the eyes near the nose. From the middle of the 19th century until the 1880s many dolls' heads had a fine red line above the eye to give greater depth to the eyelid area.

China headed doll, centre part, hair style in long moulded curls. Red line above eyes. Bottom of ear lobes exposed.

Flat top, painted side curls, eight curls at back of head. Original clothes. *Courtesy Doll & Toy Collection, Brisbane*

A few dolls' heads were made with glass eyes and these dolls are rather rare. Produced in many sizes and variations of hairstyles, the glazed china heads were sold to be joined commercially to bodies of cloth or wood. Other heads were sold separately to the home market for women to manufacture by hand or machine cloth bodies to suit the dolls' heads.

The china dolls' heads that were manufactured in the middle of last century are often found on cloth bodies, with cloth legs with sewn on fine leather boots, and leather arms with stitched leather fingers.

Other dolls with china heads and limbs of the finest quality were joined to simple jointed wooden bodies. Wooden pegs were inserted into the sewing holes in the shoulderplate head, thus connecting the head to the wooden torso. The same type of small wooden plugs were also used to join the wooden arms and legs at the elbows and knees so that they were fully movable. A china doll's head on a jointed wooden body is normally more valuable than a china headed doll on a cloth body, except if the doll's hairstyle is very elaborate.

Prior to 1870, nearly all commercially produced doll bodies were fashioned by hand. After this type the cloth bodies were sewn by machine and the stitches on these dolls are fine and evenly spaced.

On early body versions, the wooden or china arms usually had spoonlike hands, and legs that had simply modelled feet with flat soled shoes. In the latter part of last century and early this century, doll bodies had china arms with cupped hands, and legs with fancy high heeled moulded

Small low brow, china head, painting rather poor, particularly eyes, probably early this century.

Flat top, china head, hair swept to side, light pink lustre to glaze. *Private collection, Taree NSW*

Flat top glazed china headed doll, spade hands, original clothes. *Author's collection*

shoes. Many of these legs were quite bulbous, with painted blue garters, or had simulated fancy stockings.

Because there were so few male (men or boys) china heads made, china heads with short moulded hairstyles were used for dolls dressed to represent either a male or a female.

China headed dolls should be kept in their original costume whenever possible, as the doll and its costume reflect an era now gone, especially in regard to the style and materials used in the costume.

Unfortunately the original clothing may be in a bad state of disrepair and you may wish to change the clothing so that the doll can take her place with your other dolls.

Make a copy of the original clothes, using materials and style as near as possible to the original in which to display the doll. Do not throw the old clothes away, but store them in acid free tissue paper, and if you ever sell your doll, these remnants of her original clothes should be sold with the doll.

Should you have a china headed doll without clothes, study photographs of this kind of doll and their clothing which can be found in many doll reference books such as this one. Remember that the dress bodice on these dolls was normally tight fitting, emphasising the waist, and that the clothes were often sewn onto the doll.

By the turn of the century the popularity of the china headed doll was decreasing with the availability of the more childlike bisque headed doll, but manufacture of the smaller sized china headed doll continued into the first decades of the 20th century.

German Manufacturers of China Dolls

The following porcelain factories are known to have manufactured china headed dolls and/or bathing dolls, Frozen Charlottes or Bathing Beauties in Germany from the middle of last century until the years before World War II. The names that have an asterisk in front of them are featured with their factories' history in the Bisque section of this book.

* Alt, Beck & Gottschalck Nauendorf
1860 Manufactured black china dolls.
1885 Were making all china black dolls in six sizes.
1888 By this time were making dolls heads with moulded hair and also bonnet heads. They were made with painted or glass eyes and were available in 25 sizes from 1 cm to 20 cm high. They made bathing dolls until 1920.
* Bahr & Proschild Ohrdruf
1905 Manufacturing bathing dolls.
Bandorf & Co Beutelsdorf
1893–1913 Bathing dolls and swimming dolls.
Buchhold Max Lauscha
1913 Bathing dolls were advertised.
1920 Made bathing dolls, including dolls with bonnet heads, stiff bodies and moveable arms. Exported to North and South America, England, India and Australia.
Conta & Bohme Possneck
1804 Ernst Conta and Christian Gotthelf Bohme purchased the factory from Albert of Gera.
1880 Won First Prize with their display of china dolls at the World Exhibition in Melbourne.

1893 Max, Herman & Robert Conta were joint owners. Produced bathing dolls and dolls' heads with moulded hair.

1913–23 Still producing bathing dolls.

1937 Porcelain factory was shut down.

Their trademark, a knight's arm with a sword contained within a shield, can often be found under the feet of bathing or Frozen Charlotte dolls. These dolls sometimes have a clenched fist with a hole inside.

Eichorn, Christian & Sohne Steinbach

Manufactured porcelain dolls' heads, bathing dolls and doll parts until the 1930s.

Galluba & Hoffman Ilmenau

1910 Small china fashion dolls that could be naturally arranged into 5 o'clock tea groups.

1930 Bathing Beauties.

* **Goebel F & W** Oeslau

1908 Bathing dolls.

Hertwig & Co Katzhutte

1888 Exported bathing dolls to Australia. Shoulderplate bonnet head dolls and flower and butterfly type hats on shoulderplate dolls. Heads were often marked just 'Germany'.

1910 Produced bathing dolls.

1913 Made bathing dolls.

Hertwig and Co made the named china headed dolls that have Helen, Agnes, Marion, Esther, Pauline, Mabel, Dorothy and Bertha on the front of their shoulderplates.

* **Kestner** Wallendorf

Produced bathing dolls 1888, 1893, 1915, 1921, 1925. Bathing Beauties were made in 1925.

* **Kling C. F. & Co** Ohrdruf

Bathing dolls 1886, 1893, 1911, 1913, 1926. Shoulderplate moulded hair styles—1894.

Kister A.W. Fr. Schwarzburg

Bathing dolls 1877, 1888, 1893, 1906, 1913, 1920. Tea cosy dolls and bathing dolls were still being offered for sale in 1949.

Kloster Veilsdorf Veilsdorf

1893 Produced bathing dolls.

1898 Leipzig Fair—displayed bathing dolls, nanking dolls.

1909 Bathing dolls, dolls' heads.

1913 Produced dolls' heads, bathing dolls and cloth dolls.

1920 Produced dolls' heads, bathing dolls, employed 800 workers and operated 13 kilns.

1927 Porcelain bathing dolls, porcelain jointed dolls.

1930 Bathing figures and bathing dolls.

1949 Were still offering bathing dolls, dolls and dolls' heads.

Kloster Veilsdorf was one of the largest porcelain factories for the doll industry. Factory produced china heads in 5 sizes from 5–14 cm (2″–5½″), bathing dolls mould No. 900—7 cm (2¾″) and jointed dolls No. 532.

Königliche Porzellan Manufaktur—K.P.M.

BERLIN China heads of ladies and boys were made in the Berlin factory between 1840 and 1850. They were marked on the inside with the K.P.M. mark.

MEISSEN First known to have manufactured dolls' heads from 1836. On the inside of the dolls' heads are handwritten numbers and the crossed swords mark of Meissen china.

Orben, Knabe & Co Geschwenda

1909 Manufactured china heads—low brow. Marked O.K.

Small glazed china head doll with blonde hair, original clothes.

Glazed china headed doll, original costume of small checked pink cotton. *Doll & Toy Collection, Brisbane*

Parian type head, blonde moulded hair in 'Highland Mary' style. Unglazed arms and legs. Original chemise. *Author's collection*

Some of the heads were pink lustre.

Pfeiffer, Fritz Gotha

1893 Porcelain dolls' heads, Frozen Charlottes.

1897 Bathing dolls.

1913 Swimming and moveable bathing dolls.

1927 Still advertising bathing dolls.

Schlaggenwald Bohemia

Manufactured china headed dolls—Lippert & Haas owners till 1876. Had an 'S' mark impressed on inside of shoulder for Schlaggenwald, also can be a horizontal S near a number. Some heads with separate wigs had a black spot for a pate. These shoulderplate heads generally had three holes at both the back and front of the shoulderplate.

1831 Employed over 300 people.

Parian & Parian Type

Parian is the name used by many doll collectors to describe an unglazed china head with a matt white finish. The only colouring on the head is the lips, eyes, eyebrows, cheeks and hair.

Blonde was the colour used for most of the moulded hairstyles found on these dolls, but the colour varied greatly from a light cream to a tawny yellow. On some of the parian dolls the moulded hairstyle was given a clear lustre glaze to emphasise the hair contours.

Made from the 1850s until the 1880s, these dolls were mainly the product of a few German porcelain factories.

Parian type head, short blonde moulded hairstyle. This type of head was often used to represent a boy or man. Dressed in original Scottish costume. 30 cm (12"). *Courtesy Jacki Brooks*

Parian type head, moulded blonde hairstyle, dressed in original Scottish costume. *Toowoomba, Queensland*

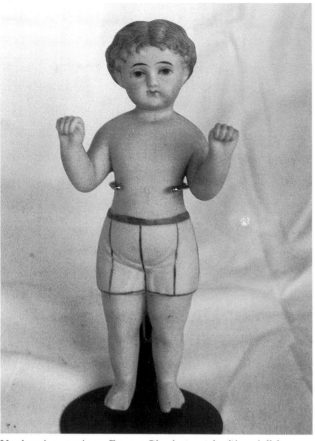

Unglazed or parian—Frozen Charlotte or bathing doll has moulded and painted trunks. *Private collection, Brisbane*

'Bonnet head' blonde bisque doll head, with moulded hair, hat and bodice. *Devonport, Tasmania*

Belton type head, unglazed china, fine colouring, original clothes. *Private collection, Brisbane*

Moulded blonde hairstyle, blonde bisque head, original clothes, very light colouring. *Private collection, Queensland*

Tea-cosy or half doll, 9 cm (3½″) tall. *Private collection, Brisbane*

There are hundreds of different styles and types of these unglazed heads, and they come with every imaginable adornment, from flowers, snood, ruffles, plumes, jewellery, ribbons and feathers. The more exquisite of these heads have some of the detail picked out in gold lustre.

Not only the moulded hair had added decoration, but many of the heads were decorated on the actual shoulder-plate as well, with moulded necklaces, bodices, collars, etc.

The eyes were generally painted blue with black irises on these doll heads, although on some of the highest quality heads inserted eyes were used. Parian, tinted bisque and glazed china heads were often made using the same mould, the only variation in the heads was the way the head was finished in colour and whether it was glazed or unglazed. Bodies of cloth, normally filled with sawdust, are found in conjunction with parian heads.

The main manufacturers of these miniature art forms, and also the tinted bisque heads, were Alt, Beck & Gottschalck, Hertwig & Co. and C. F. Kling, with a few made by Kestner.

Half doll. Pin cushion. *Author's collection*

Parian head, blonde moulded hair, centre part, fine features, original body, narrow waist. *Hervey Bay, Queensland*

Fine quality parian head, with elaborate blonde hairstyle, ornamented with fine gilded band across head.

Unusual glazed china doll. Head is strung to body so head can move. *Author's collection*

Glazed china, Art Deco head.

Half doll with legs—pin cushion. *Private collection, Brisbane*

Half doll or tea-cosy doll as crumb brush. *Author's collection*

Half doll on base representing a rose. *Private collection, Brisbane*

Selection of Frozen Charlottes or bathing dolls. Largest is 15 cm. *Author's collection*

Tinted Bisque or Blonde Bisque (2nd grade Parian)

A tinted bisque head is actually the same type of head as a parian head, the main difference is that the head, except for the hair, has an overall pink blush. This pink gives the doll's head a much more natural appearance than the starkness of the parian head.

Pink Lustre

Name given to a tinted bisque head that has been glazed. Once this has been done, the head colouring has a much greater depth and lifelike appearance than a normal white china head. Some of the pink lustre heads have wigs, others can be found with a brown coloured hairstyle instead of the stark black of the white glazed head. Pink lustre was sometimes used on the busts of telephone dolls or tea cosy dolls.

Tea Cosy Dolls

These small representations of the bust of a human figure, mainly females, first became popular in 1918, and there was no material too expensive or luxurious enough, when first introduced, to serve the purpose of the skirt of a tea-cosy doll's costume.

These glazed china busts, usually depicting a woman from the waist up, were manufactured in all manner of period costumes and hairstyles from Madame Dubarry to flappers. The base of the 'dolls' were sewn on to the tea-cosy doll base, or in other instances, crumb brushes or handkerchief sachets. Because of the sewn skirts of the bases of the teacosies, these busts were quickly given the definition of 'dolls'.

These busts, half dolls or tea-cosy dolls, depending on where you are from, have often over the years been turned into works of art by the skilful hands of creative women, knitting or crocheting their often voluminous skirts, to serve a practical and mundane use, that of keeping a teapot warm.

Frozen Charlottes—Bathing Dolls

Frozen Charlottes or bathing dolls were manufactured in simple two piece moulds using china clay and then most of them were glazed.

The first bathing dolls (or Badekinder) were naked with a universal hairstyle (thus representing either sex) or were completely bald. The arms of these glazed one piece dolls were either moulded across the chest or close to the side of the body.

Later the arms were extended from the side or were bent with the hands pointing forward. Moulded hair, bonnets or wigs were added to these usually toddler type one piece dolls.

To give them a more child-like appearance moulded clothes were added, but most of these dolls kept their overall shiny whiteness. Colour crept into the moulded clothes with a few becoming quite decorate and highly detailed. Most of the dolls were left plain white or had short hairstyles painted to represent a young boy (some were even sexed), with painted eyes and simple features.

Frozen Charlottes, Badekinder or bathing dolls were manufactured in their multitudes by nearly every German porcelain factory and ranged in size from 2 cm (¾") to over 38 cm (15").

Bathing Beauty. *Author's collection*

Bathing Beauty, glazed china. *Armidale*

Other Countries Manufacturing China Dolls/Heads

Australia

During the early years of World War I when china dolls' heads were hard to get, some enterprising employeès of Dinmore Pottery near Ipswich, Queensland, started to manufacture dolls' heads. They were made of a white earthenware china and glazed to look like German china headed dolls. Rather crude by comparison, they were quite acceptable to a doll starved child. All the heads I have so far seen and been able to examine have been men's or boys' heads with black or brown painted hair.

When in Ballarat in 1985, I was told that there were some unusual white china dolls dug up around the Ballarat region, that are distinctly different from those known to be of German origin. Are these the work of some long forgotten small porcelain factory here in Australia?

Denmark

Royal Copenhagen Manufactury 1843–1860, 1977 +
Produced about 23,000 china dolls' heads of very high quality from around 1843 until 1860. These heads were marked with three lines inside the breastplate.

1977 Three of the original moulds were used by the factory to remake china heads similar in colour and painting to those manufactured last century. Two of the shoulder-heads were of a lady with moulded dark brown hair in a knot at the back of the head. Made in 14 cm (5½") and 9.5 cm (3¾"). Also in the 9.5 cm (3¾") size was a boy's

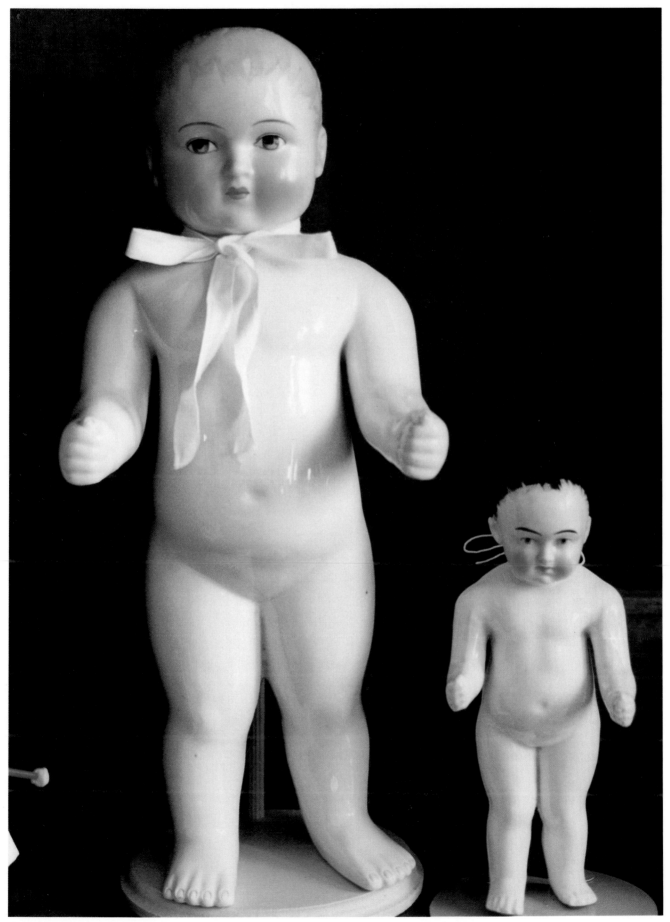

Large 'pink lustre' bathing dolls or Frozen Charlottes. *Private collection, Sydney*

Glazed heads made at Dinmore Pottery, Ipswich, Queensland during World War I.

Short bob glazed head, 1920s style.

head that had moulded tan hair with a side part. All heads had three sewing holes on the back and front of the shoulderplate. The heads were marked inside along the back edge of the shoulder—"Denmark" in green and a mould number.

France
Bawo & Dotter Bavaria, New York and Limoges, France
1896 Established a white china factory at Limoges, France.
Made china limbs and china heads. Mark B & D incised.
D'Autremont Paris
Name found on some china headed dolls with kid bodies.
Jacob Petit France
1840–1860 One of the few French doll manufacturers who made his own fine china dolls' heads instead of importing them from Germany. These heads are usually characterised by a delicately modelled face and eight sewing holes on the shoulderplate. Sometimes the heads can be found glazed on the inside as well as the outside. Marks painted on the shoulders are PAR BREVET, J P or 10 J P.
Sèvres France
China dolls' heads were manufactured at Sèvres during World War I.

Sweden
Rostrand Porcelain Factory Sweden
1868 Advertised that they sold dolls' heads, arms and legs in their catalogue. By 1900 their heads were poured, earlier heads had been pressed into moulds. Mark—generally a red 'R' inside the head, under the glaze, or a letter and a single number on the outside of the head to the side front of the shoulderplate.

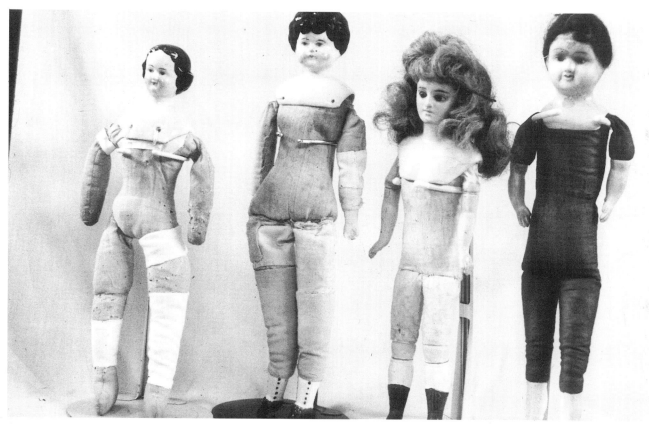

Bodies from left to right: (a) Simple cotton body, several times repaired—head 1830-1840. (b) China arms, low brow china head, moulded china shoes and spats. (c) Fine wax covering over composition head, glass eyes, composition arms and moulded boots and stockings. (d) Green nankin body, unglazed head with wig, unglazed arms and legs.

Simple unglazed china doll's house doll. *Private collection, Brisbane*

Bathing dolls, Frozen Charlottes or Badekinder dolls. The small one on the right could have been used as a favour in a Christmas pudding. Faint traces can be seen of their once painted hairstyles. The small doll on the left has a moulded hat and simple moulded clothing. *Author's collection*

ALL BISQUE, GERMANY Fully jointed, original clothes, painted eyes, 6 cm (2½″). *Author's collection*

ALL BISQUE, One piece head and torso, original clothes, painted eyes. *Private collection, Toowomba, Queensland*

Bisque Dolls

A. L. & Cie see Lanternier, A.L. (France)

Alexandre, Henri Paris 1889–91
Henri Alexandre made bisque headed dolls from 1889. In 1892 he was succeded by Tourrel. By 1895 Tourrel had merged with Jules Steiner, also in Paris.

★93

Alexandre was the designer of the Bébé Phénix dolls and one of the three manufacturers who used either Bébé Phénix or Phénix Bébé as a trademark over the years. Besides the Bébé Phénix he also made other dolls, many of which bore

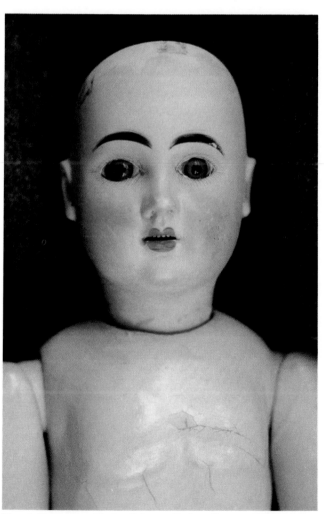

Henri Alexandre, Paris. *Private collection, Kempsey NSW. Photograph courtesy Wilga Hughes*

his trademark of an incised number and also a five-pointed star. In 1889 dolls bearing the Alexandre trademark were displayed at the Paris Exposition.

All bisque Germany, France 1880–1930s, Japan 1910–50s
A general term used to describe a doll that is completely made of bisque porcelain. These small dolls, ranging from 1″ (2.5 cm) to 8″ or 9″ (20–22.5 cm) in height, were manufactured in abundance by many German and French firms from the 1880s until the 1930s. Japan was also a manufacturer this century but the dolls were not of the high quality found in European dolls. Early Japanese dolls bear the word NIPPON. These small dolls were sold as play dolls, dressed in ethnic costume and sold as souvenirs, and used to people dolls' houses. Around 1906 they were very popular as birthday cake decorations.

German manufacturers include Alt, Beck & Gottschalck·who made dolls with moulded clothes as well as the famous Baby Bo Kaye. Other manufacturers were Bahr & Proschild (whose dolls included Snow Babies), Hertwig & Co. (moulded clothes and hair), Gebruder Heubach, Kestner (all bisque Bye-Lo) and Simon & Halbig.

France also made these small dolls (often exquisite minute examples of their larger dolls), with S.F.B.J. and Unis France being two of the better known makers.

Japan, particularly in the depression years of the 1930s, made cheap all bisque dolls with a much more porous finish, paler and whiter in colour than the French and German dolls. These white poor quality dolls are now often referred to as 'stone bisque'.

Unfortunately many of these dolls are unmarked, others with only country of origin. Some though have numbers and initials which help to identify some of their manufacturers. The format of these dolls can vary considerably, but the most simple way to categorise them is as follows:

(1) German manufacture
(2) French manufacture
(3) Japanese manufacture.

Within the scope of these three countries you will find dolls made thus:

(i) Fully jointed—head, arms and legs, either strung with rubber, wired or peg jointed through the body
(ii) One piece head and torso, moveable arms and legs—wired, strung or peg jointed
(iii) One piece head, torso and legs with moveable arms only
(iv) All one piece.

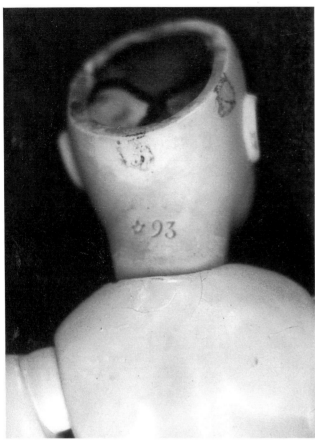

Marking on back, Henri Alexandre bisque head. *Private collection, Kempsey NSW. Photograph courtesy Wilga Hughes*

ALL BISQUE, Japan. All one piece, moulded clothes. *Author's collection*

ALL BISQUE, Sleeping glass eyes, all original, 11 cm (4¼″). *Private collection, Tasmania*

ALL BISQUE, Germany. One piece head, torso and legs; moulded hat. *Private collection, NSW*

ALL BISQUE, Painted eyes. *Private collection, Queensland*

ALL BISQUE, Moulded hair, original clothes, 10 cm (4″). *Private collection, Tasmania*

ALL BISQUE, Bent limb baby, all original, painted eyes, 5 cm (2″). *Private collection, Tasmania*

ALL BISQUE, Bare feet, moulded clothes. *Private collection, Devonport, Tasmania*

ALL BISQUE, 1920s moulded shoes, all original. *Private collection, Tasmania*

ALL BISQUE, All bisque dolls, moulded clothes. *Private collection, Tasmania*

ALL BISQUE, Germany. All original clothes. Doll on left, glass eyes. Doll on right, painted eyes. *Private collection, Tasmania*

The above four types of bodies can be found with:

(a) Sleeping or fixed glass eyes
(b) Painted eyes
(c) Belton type head—wigged, or pate with wig, or moulded hair [particularly applies to those in categories (iii) and (iv)]
(d) Bent or straight limbs—denoting baby or child/girl
(e) Bare feet
(f) Painted, moulded socks and shoes or boots
(g) Moulded clothes [mainly found in categories (iii) and (iv)].

Alt, Beck & Gottschalck Nauendorf near Coburg, Germany c. 1880-1941, porcelain factory

ALL BISQUE, Japan. All original. Large dolls, glass eyes. Small dolls, painted eyes. *Private collection*

1880 c. Bisque shoulder heads, with moulded hair and sometimes hats. Either with painted or glass eyes, closed mouth, cloth bodies, bisque lower limbs, mould numbers 890, 990, 1000, 1008, 1028, 1064, 1142, 1254, 1288.
1882 First known to have exported dolls.
1885 c. Bisque turned shoulder plate heads, wigged, glass sleeping or set eyes, closed mouth. Gussetted kid body, bisque lower arms. Mould numbers 639, 698 (open or closed mouth), 1123, 1235. After 1888 these numbers could be found in conjunction with DEP.

Alt, Beck & Gottschalck. Mould no. A.B.G./1361/55. *L. Hurford collection*

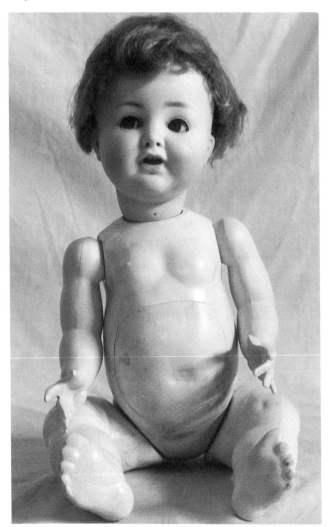

A.B.G. on composition bent limb body. *Private collection*

1890 Two factories employing 300 workers as well as 100 families working at home.
A child doll was made with bisque head, wig, sleeping eyes, open mouth, ball jointed body. Mould number 1362.

1910 + Character dolls with bisque heads, wig, sleeping eyes, open mouth, some with open nostrils, on composition bodies. Mould numbers 1322, 1352, 1357, 1361.

1911 All bisque girl dolls. Numbers 100, 125, 150 and 225 often in conjunction with other numbers. These dolls have glass eyes, open/closed mouth, wigs, moulded white stockings, blue garters, black shoes and a chubby body.

1920s Manufactured mainly for the USA market; among the most famous:
Bye-Lo Baby, designed by Grace Storey Putnam
Baby Bo Kaye, designed by J. L. Kallus

1926 Bonnie Babe, designed by Georgene Averill.

1930 'Albego' was used as part of their mould mark— designates the doll's head was made between 1930 and 1940.

1941 Documentation that they were still producing bisque dolls.

A.M. (Armand Marseille) see Marseille, Armand

Amberg, Louis & Son New York USA, importer with branch in Sonneberg Germany
This American firm is most famous for the importation of the New Born Babe, a model of a baby only a few weeks old. Nearly all the other Thuringia factories copied this type of doll and they were an instant export success. The name New Born Babe was registered by Louis Amberg in 1914, for a doll designed by Jeno Juszko, but documentation and reports suggest it came onto the market c. 1925. The doll was made by Theodor Recknagel, mould number 886.

L.A.&.S.

Marks: © L.A. & S. 1914 G 45520 Germany # 4
Heads copyrighted by LOUIS AMBERG and Son
© L. Amberg & Son Germany 886/2

Bahr & Proschild. *Private collection, Sydney*

Baby Bo Kaye designed by J.L. Kallus. Bisque head manufactured for the US Market by Alt, Beck & Gottschalck. *Lesley Hurford collection*

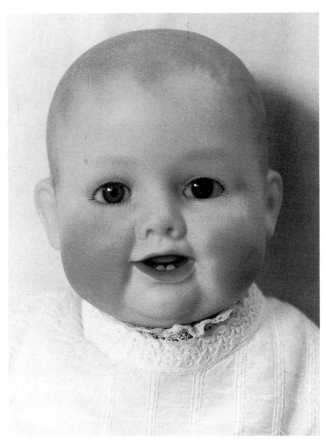

Bonnie Babe, copyright Georgene Averill, Germany. Bisque head manufactured by Alt, Beck & Gottschalck. Mark 1005/3652 2/0. *Private collection, Queensland*

A.B.G. Toddler, 'Starfish' hands. *Lesley Hurford collection*

Bisque head manufactured by Max Oscar Arnold for Welsch & Co., composition body, 48 cm (19″). Mark MOA/A200/Welsch/Germany/3

American doll manufacturers/wholesalers who used German bisque heads

Louis Amberg: New Born Baby—made by Theodor Recknagel
   Baby Peggy—Armand Marseille
Geo. Borgfeldt & Co.: Bonnie Babe—Alt, Beck & Gottschalck
   Just Me—Armand Marseille
Century Doll Co.: Heads made by Kestner
Hamburger & Co.: Dolly Dimple—Gebr. Heubach
   Registered such names as Santa, Old Glory, Viola, found on bisque heads.
Horsman E. & I.: Tiny Babe
Arranbee: My Dream Baby by Armand Marseille
   Simon & Halbig heads in conjunction with Arranbee markings.

Arena, Felix 1918-20
One of the lesser known makers of bisque headed dolls; his trademark 'Mignon' was registered in France for use on dolls' heads. Felix Arena was joined by Michael Lafond in 1920.

Arnold, Max Oscar Neustadt near Coburg, Germany 1888-1931, porcelain and doll factory
1877 Founded.
1888 Participated in World Fair, Exhibition Building, Melbourne, receiving prize for elegant doll suits.
1903 Registered a walking doll.
1903-08 Registered Ma-mas in dolls.
1909 The singing talking doll, which was approx. 75 cm (29½") tall.

1910 Necessary gramophone rolls for above doll were produced in their own factory.
1919 Purchased Gebr. Knock, doll manufacturers.

1920 Dolls bearing MOA and Welsch were produced in the MOA factory for Welsch & Co. of Sonneberg.
1931 Factory sold to Phillip Rosenthal.
Dolls have bisque socket heads, wigs, set or sleeping eyes, open mouths, ball jointed bodies with the markings MOA and Welsch. Mould numbers 150 or 200.

A.S.
Dolls with these initials were made by either Arthur Schoenau of Sonneberg or August Steiner of Koppelsdorf. For further information see Schoenau, Arthur or Steiner, August.

Shoulderplate with kid body, manufactured by Max Oscar Arnold for Welsch & Co. Mark MOA/250.1/W & C/ Germany

Australian companies that used German bisque heads
It is documented that the following Australian firms imported German bisque heads in the 1930s for use in manufacturing dolls for the Australian market:

Laurie Cohen of Sydney NSW imported flange necked bisque heads, mainly by Armand Marseille. Some of the mould numbers known to have been used are 341, 351, 352, 382, 384. These dolls had cloth bodies and celluloid arms and legs imported from Japan. The Australian made bodies were marked with the L.C. Hush-a-bye shield and names such as Betty and Sally. Judith Anne was stamped on the front of the body of dolls for David Jones, a large department store in Sydney.

Hoffnungs, wholesalers of Sydney NSW, also imported flange neck bisque heads, mainly by Armand Marseille. Known mould numbers are 341 and 351. These dolls were amongst many sold by Hoffnungs under the I-Doll label. The cloth bodies were made by Vera Kent who used celluloid full arms and legs from Japan to complete the doll assembly.

Shoulderplate heads, Brisbane, presumed pre-World War II

Two head moulds used by Melbourne Pram Factory to make bisque heads during World War I

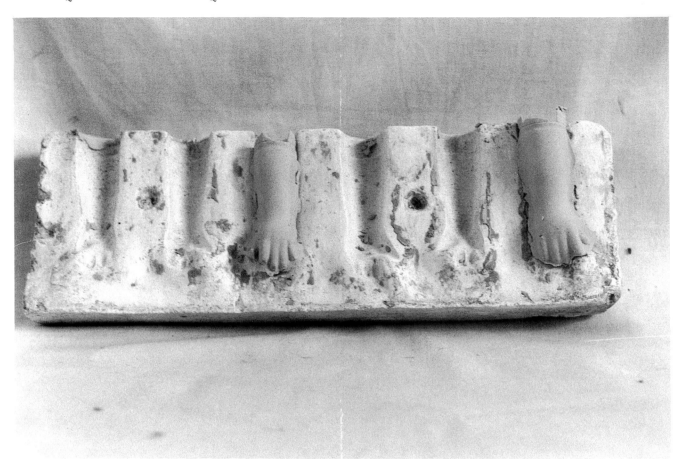

Half an arms mould used by Melbourne Pram Factory. Three pairs of arms were poured at a time

Half a legs mould used by Melbourne Pram Factory. Two pairs of legs were poured at a time

Australian manufacturers of bisque heads

It is now kmown that the following made dolls with a bisque—like head:

Melbourne Pram Factory—during the First World War. Shoulderplate heads manufactured in Brisbane—maker unknown.

Automata

Man's secret wish was always to make an inanimate object move. Watchmakers at European courts in the 18th century were ordered to develop objects that moved by means of forces hidden in their interior. Many of these mechanical marvels were commandeered by kings and princes and demonstrated in the evenings for ladies' entertainment.

The industrial revolution brought a change to Automatas with many inventions, as well as simplification of movement, cheaper manufacturing cost and mass production.

French manufacturers such as Decamps, Alexander Theroude and Leopold Lambert played a leading role in the history of Automatas, but their ideas were shamelessly copied by Sonneberg dollmakers who further simplified the functions and methods of production. This led to cheaper renditions of this popular parlour toy of the Victorian and early Edwardian era.

The category Automata should only be applied to dolls that perfectly imitate human actions and movement. Others such as mechanical walking dolls, phonograph dolls, etc., are semi-automatas or moveable dolls.

Unfortunately many collectors have a tendency to date bisque head automatas much too early, for although a great number of these delightful dolls were produced in the latter half of last century, firms such as Decamps and Leopold Lambert continued their models well into the 20th century.

Autoperipatetikos 1862 + Martin & Runyon, New York USA

Patented on 15 July 1862 by Enoch Rice Morrison, these wind-up mechanical walking dolls with kid arms were approximately 10″ (25.5 cm) tall. They had an intricate

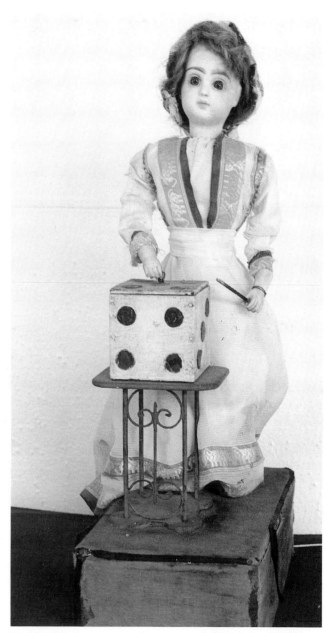

Armand Marseille 352 bisque head on Laurie Cohen body, Sydney 1932 + . *Author's collection*

'Devil's Dice' Automata, Jumeau head. Dice is in closed position before mechanism is wound. *Newstead House, Brisbane*

'Devil's Dice' Automata after the clockwork mechanism has been activated, the doll's head has moved and the lid of the box lifted. At the first lift the box appears empty, the lid closes, the left arm taps the dice thrice, the lid lifts and the devil's head appears, the lid closes and the sequence ends.

walking mechanism with metal feet that protruded through a round flat wooden base. A cardboard underskirt concealed the mechanism and also acted as a hoop for the fabric overskirt. The English version, distributed by J. Peacock, dollmaker of London, had a much more slender cardboard skirt.

Shoulderplate heads of china, parian, painted cloth, papier mâché and bisque were among the various heads used on the bodies of these dolls. Bisque heads were used by E. Barrios, France for the French version.

Averill, Madame Georgene USA 1915–40s

1915 Used trade name Madame Hendren until early 1920s when name stayed with the Averill Manufacturing Co. when sold.

1923 Georgene Averill with Madame Georgene Inc. and Georgene Novelty Co. until World War II.

1926 Bonnie Babe—a smiling bisque headed doll designed by Georgene Averill and made by Alt, Beck & Gottschalk. The cloth bodies were made by K & K Toy Co. and were distributed by Geo. Borgfeldt, New York. The dolls' heads had moulded hair, sleeping glass eyes, open mouth, two lower teeth and a flange neck. Mould number could be 1368 or 1402.

An all bisque Bonnie Babe was also made but was unmarked except for paper label on stomach.

Baby Bo Kaye 1926–28

Baby Bo Kaye was the trade name for a doll designed by Joseph L. Kallus. It was distributed by Geo. Borgfeldt in the United States. The bisque head with moulded hair and glass eyes was on a 'Mama' type cloth body with slender composition legs. The dolls were also produced with celluloid heads made in Germany, as well as composition.

Bahr & Proschild Ohrdruf, Germany 1871–1918, porcelain factory

1871 Firm founded; known to have made bisque heads with mould numbers only, in the early 1870s. Made bisque heads, all bisque dolls and bathing dolls.

1880 c. Belton type heads, paperweight eyes, closed mouth, pierced ears, composition and wood bodies. Mould numbers 204, 224.

1888 + Socket heads, sleeping eyes, open mouth, ball jointed bodies with mould numbers 224, 239, 273, 275, 277, 297, 325, 379, 394. Shoulderplate heads, sleeping eyes, open mouth, kid body. Mould numbers 246, 309.

1894 Employed 200 workers.

1905 Advertised bisque dolls' heads, babies, bathing dolls.

1910 c. Character child doll, ball jointed body. Mould numbers 536, 2072. Character Baby—composition body.

Autoperipatetikos. This mechanical walking doll (with her box) has a composition head, but these dolls can be found with china and bisque heads also. *Courtesy Entally House, Tasmania*

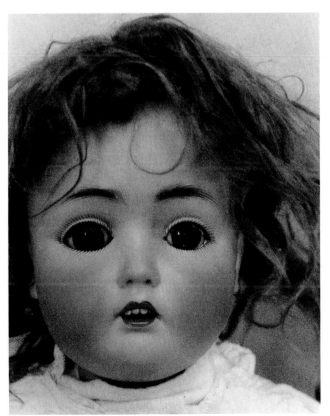

264-S   Bahr & Proschild

Bahr & Proschild, 585, size 2/0. *Private collection, Queensland*

All original Bahr & Proschild 585, size 0. *Lesley Hurford collection*

Mould numbers 585, 604, 624, 678, 619, 614. These dolls had a socket head, solid dome or pate with wig, sleeping eyes, bent limb body.

1918 Factory bought by Bruno Schmidt, and B & P emblem was incorporated with the heart insignia of Bruno Schmidt.

Bahr and Proschild heads are sometimes mistakenly identified as French because of being found on typically 'French' bodies.

Over the years Bahr & Proschild used a variety of different trademarks, and here is a list to help in date identification.

From 1888—dep mark
1895—B & P
1900—B & P and crossed swords
1919—B & P with a heart shape, after Bruno Schmidt of Walterhausen bought the factory.

Bahr & Proschild can also be found spelt Baehr & Proeschild.

Barrois, Madame E. Paris, France 1860–70s, doll factory
One of the earliest manufacturers to use porcelain dolls'

E. Barrois, French Fashion. Painted eyes, kid body

heads in France. These heads were used for Autoperipate-tikos dolls and also for dolls dressed in ethnic costumes, poupards and fashion dolls.

£ B

It is known that she also purchased heads from unidentified French and German factories for her doll making. The bodies were of cloth or kid.

Bartenstein, Fritz Huttensteinach, Germany 1880–1905, inventor and factory owner
1877 Advertised two-faced dolls; one face was serene, the other crying, and the faces could be changed by turning the doll's head within the hood that normally covered the back of the head. Many factories copied this mechanism which, when one of two threads was drawn, turned the head to either side, at the same time initiating a voice calling 'Mama' or 'Papa'.

Bathing Beauties 1920+
Small figures of bathing beauties, similar to knickknacks. First sold in 1920, they were produced by almost all the porcelain factories of Thuringia. Some were depicted nude, but most were decorously draped or had moulded bathing suits.

532 bisque head manufactured by Bahr & Proschild for Kley & Hahn

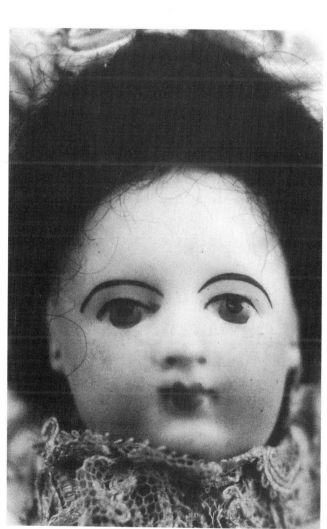

Barrois, France. Fashion doll, painted eyes

French Bébé. Small bisque headed doll ball jointed, made in France

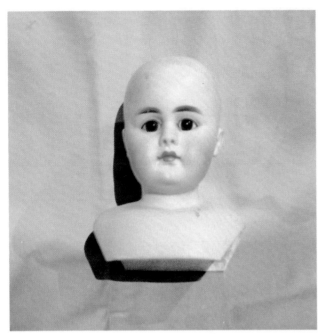

Belton type head, unmarked, shoulder plate, glass eyes.
Queensland

Bathing Dolls Sometimes called **Badekinder** or **Frozen Charlottes**

These stiff, one piece dolls when properly made and placed in water do not sink, but are able to lie in a horizontal position on the water. For dolls to do this they had to be made of the best quality slip. Very small bathing dolls, usually sold cheaply, were not poured but pressed. This method was fast and clean and left no visible seams. The smallest of these dolls were just 1 cm (less than ½″), the largest 50 cm (19½″). The large size dolls were used by children at the seaside. The small ones were exported to Australia, England and the United States to become favours in cakes and puddings—hence the other common name for them, Pudding Dolls.

Bébé

This is a generic term often used for describing a doll of childlike proportions of French manufacture from the period 1880–1890s. Bébé dolls have bisque heads and well shaped bodies of either kid or ball jointed wood and/or composition.

Among the most famous makers of Bébés are Bru, Jumeau and Jules Steiner.

French Bébé, A. Steiner. *Author's collection*

Belton type head, shoulderplate, painted eyes. *Tamworth, NSW*

Bébé Phénix see also Phénix Bébé 1889–1902
A bisque headed doll with sleeping eyes, closed mouth, fully jointed body including wrists, or a straight legged walking body, in five heights from 32–53 cm (12½–21 in).

1889 Bébé Phénix was advertised by Henri Alexandre—designer and manufacturer—as being patented and registered. The word 'PHENIX' is usually found stamped in red in company with the incised trademark of a five-pointed star and number of Henri Alexandre.

1890 Alexandre advertised a series of 30 models, with light jointed composition bodies of excellent build which came dressed and undressed.

1892 Alexandre's successor, Tourrel, used the same advertisement that had appeared in 1890.

1894 Trademark Bébé Phénix was registered in France by Widow Lafosse, whose late husband had succeeded Jules Steiner as head of the Steiner company. The registration was for a walking doll with a head that moved.

1900 Jules Mettais, who had succeeded Widow Lafosse, advertised the Phénix Bébé.

Belton type head 1875 +
Although no known bisque heads are marked Belton, it is a term in common use for a particular type of domed bisque head found on women or girl dolls. These bisque heads can be flat, concave or convex on top, and sometimes have two or three holes in the pate area, which were there to assist in tying on the wig. The majority of this type of head can be found with closed mouths and set-in paperweight eyes. Bahr & Proschild made this type of head—mould numbers 204, 224. Simon & Halbig also made these heads. A small size head marked 137 is of unknown manufacture.

Berg, Herman von Koppelsdorf, Germany 1904–26 + , doll factory

H.v.B

1904 Founded factory at Huttensteinach to supply wigs for dolls and for inserting eyes.

1913 Extended workshops and moved to Koppelsdorf and traded abroad.

1918 Babies and jointed dolls became part of supplier's line.

1922 Advertised 'jointed dolls with porcelain heads'.

1925 Advertised 'the new born', an imitation of a few weeks old baby with sleeping eyes, open mouth, moveable tongue, cloth body.

1926 Further patents for refinement of New Born baby doll.

Marks: H.v.B 500/4 or H.v.B. 500/4k (socket head)

Bergmann, Charles M. Walterhausen, Germany 1888–1931, doll factory

1888 Founded factory with two workers.
Specialised in ball jointed composition bodies and bought bisque heads from companies such as Armand Marseille, Simon & Halbig and Alt, Beck & Gottschalck.

1896 Advertised 'factory of finest ball jointed child dolls'.

1900 & 1901 Took out patents for different ball jointed bodies.

1904 Used bisque shoulder heads, Simon & Halbig No. 1280, for his Columbia doll.

Herman von Berg. Mark Germany H. v. B. *Doll & Toy Collection, Brisbane*

Two faced Bergner

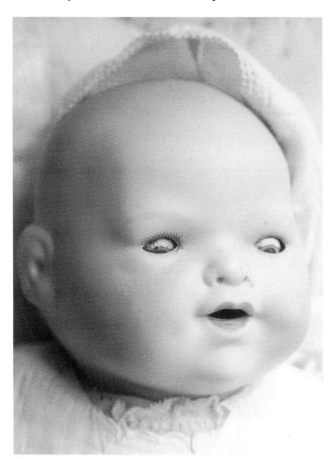
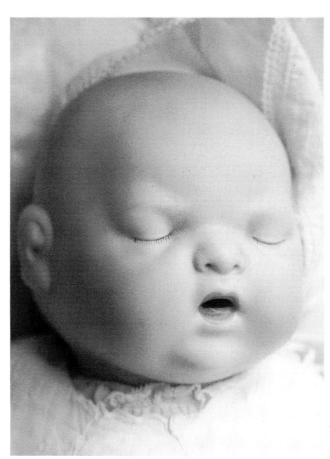

Two faced bisque headed baby by Herman von Berg. *Lesley Hurford collection*

C.M. Bergmann, mark C.M. Bergmann/Walterhausen/
Germany/1916

1914 150 workers and was producing Baby Belle and
character babies for sale in the USA.
1915 Columbia name registered for shoulder heads and
socket heads.
1918 Advertised ball jointed dolls, bent limb babies and
toddlers.
1931 Bankruptcy.
Bergmann's most important customer was L. Wolf & Co.,
New York. A distinguishing feature of most dolls found with
Bergmann's 1916 mould marking is the flat shape of the
back of the head.

C.M.Bergmann
Waltershousen
Germany
1916

Bergner, Carl Sonneberg, Germany 1860–1922 + , doll
factory

1860 The firm was founded by Carl Bergner.
1883 Founder on the committee of the Sonneberg trade-
school.
1890 Designed a doll whose head turned from side to side
by means of a spring.

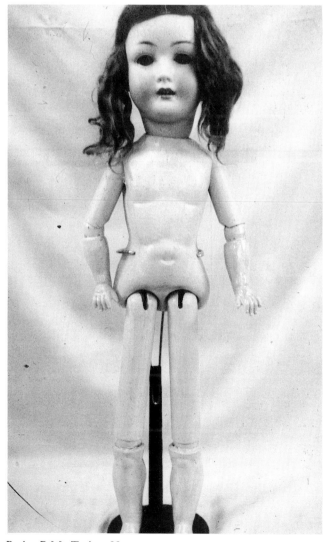

Body. P.M. Trebor 22
Notice straight upper legs—these are referred to as
'broomstick legs'. They are turned wood

Three faced doll by Carl Bergner

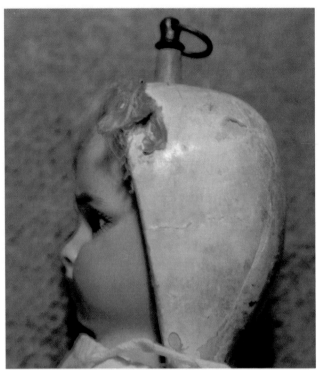

The strong papier mâché cowl that hides the other face on a multi-face doll. The head is turned by the handle on top. C. Bergner. *Private collection, Kempsey*

Doll with two faces, cowl covers one face

1893 Designed a doll who could make a sound when the upper body was turned against the lower body.
1903 Multi-faced dolls were displayed by Bergner at Leipzig Fair.
1904 Marketed a changeable face doll.
1908 The firm of Carl Bergner was incorporated in the commercial register.
1922 Multi-faced doll with laughing, crying, and sleeping face—also available in black—was advertised.
According to Dorothy Coleman, some of the bisque heads used by Carl Bergner were made by Simon & Halbig.

Bierschenck, Fritz Sonneberg, Germany 1906–27 + , doll factory and export

F.I.B

1906 Bought the doll factory of E. Escher Jnr.
1910 Registered a porcelain bisque head design.
1922 Dressed and undressed dolls were advertised.

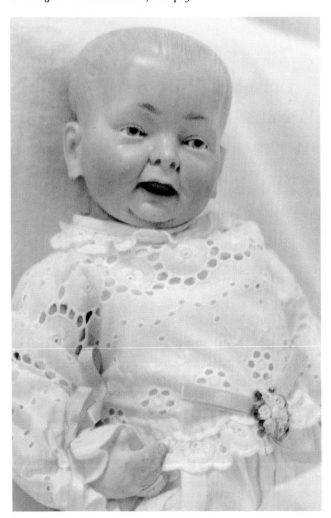

Fritz Bierschenck. *Hervey Bay, Queensland*

1926 Patented a baby doll.
1930 Production ceased.
One of the firm's big successes was dressing Kewpies produced in other porcelain factories.
In the 1920s an explosion destroyed factory buildings causing Bierschenck to go into bankruptcy.
He developed a patent to pack dolls for export. His 'neck furrow' was so successful almost all the dollmakers of Sonneberg used his system for their overseas customers.

Bisque 1850–1940s

Bisque is an unglazed, matt finished porcelain made from kaolin clay. The quality found in dolls and dolls' heads ranges from the smooth translucent bisque of the French beauties of Bru and Jumeau to the grainy variety found in cheaper examples and also in those of English and Japanese manufacture.
There were two methods of making bisque heads in the moulds.

1. Early bisque heads were made from paste which was kneaded, rolled, cut into squares and then pressed into the inside of the head mould.
2. Porcelain slip was poured into the moulds, and after a set time poured out leaving a thin walled hollow head in the mould.

When dry the head was cleaned and eyes and mouth cut out if necessary, and then it was fired in a large kiln at high temperatures for about 27 hours.
Once cool, facial features were painted and the head was fired again, this time at a lower temperature. Final touches of eyes and teeth were added, then the body was attached and hair and dress finished the doll.
Heads of bisque were produced from the 1860s with Paris, France and the Thuringia area of Germany being the primary areas of production.
The unavailability of dolls during World War I led to Japan, Britain, the USA and even Australia making bisque heads for dolls. Most were unable to compete with Germany and France after the war, particularly due to these countries' manufacture of character dolls and baby dolls in the 1920s.
Before 1880 most bisque heads were of the shoulderplate type, with or without a swivel neck. The socket neck was introduced with the invention of the ball jointed body, and the flange necked head was used for cloth bodied baby dolls.

Black/brown bisque France, Germany 1880 + , England 1914 +

Black and brown bisque headed dolls are now eagerly sought by many doll collectors. The bisque heads on these dolls have been produced by two methods.

1. Coloured slip of various hues was poured into moulds and fired; this colour is permanent.
2. The majority of coloured heads were painted after the first fire to the required shade and some were then fired again to make the colour permanent.

Many French and German firms used their regular moulds, and thus you may find a black/brown and white version of one mould, such as the 341 Dream Baby made by Armand

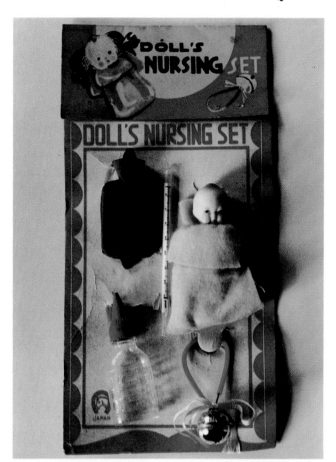

Post World War II Japanese bisque doll set. *Author's collection*

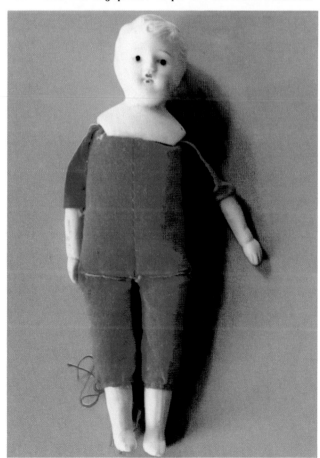

Japanese bisque headed doll, 1920s–30s. *Author's collection*

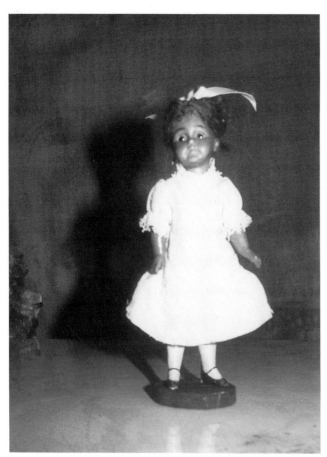

Original clothes, 23 cm (9″), mark 1079/DEP S & H.
Author's collection

Original clothes, mark Heubach Koppelsdorf 444 4/0.
Author's collection

Original clothes, mark Heubach Koppelsdorf 399 10/0.
Private collection, Taree

Heubach Koppelsdorf 344.0. *Private collection, Queensland*

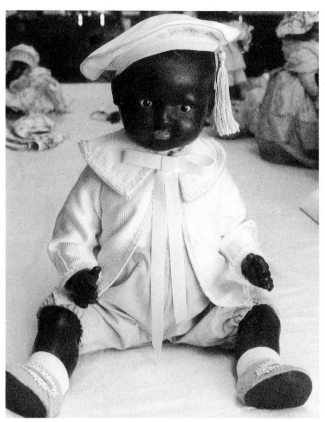

A.M. 351 composition body. *Betty Brown collection*

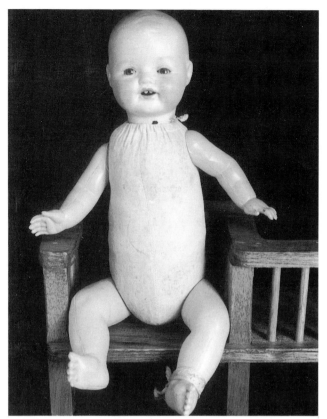

Typical four piece cloth body, celluloid arms and legs, German bisque head, marked A.M. 382. Assembled by Laurie Cohen, an Australian company that used German bisque heads. *Private collection, Gulgong NSW*

Marseille. Other firms such as Ernst Heubach designed special moulds with pronounced Negroid features.

These black/brown dolls had bodies of composition, cloth or kid that were made in colours to complement the head colour.

Known French makers were Bru, Jumeau, S.F.B.J. 60 and 226, Unis France and Steiner.

German makers included Armand Marseille 1894, 341, 351, Bahr & Proschild, Kammer & Reinhardt, Simon & Halbig 739, 949, 1039, 1249, Kestner 134; and some all bisque dolls, Heubach Koppelsdorf 399 and 444 and also made the South Sea Baby for A. Luge & Co. Many of the dark dolls featured googly eyes.

English firms such as Doll Pottery Co. also made dark coloured heads.

B.N.D. see British National Dolls Ltd, London 1933–50s.

Bodies

From the very beginning when bisque heads were first used on dolls in the 1860s until the 1940s great changes were made in doll bodies to achieve greater mobility and lessen fragility. Early Fashion dolls can be found with all kid bodies, gussetted and ungussetted, kid over jointed wood, and other variations including blown leather.

Bébé or early girl dolls had bisque heads with cloth or kid bodies, with simple gussets or no gussets at all. These were later improved to give more mobility at the elbows, hips and knees with wired hinged joints. The ball jointed body originated in France and was used by both Jumeau and Bru on their Bébés.

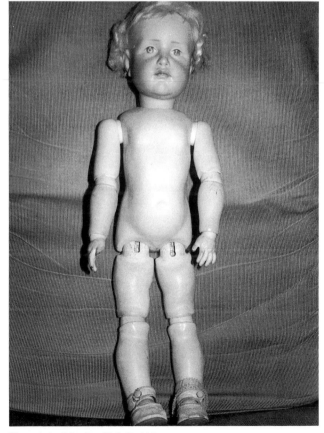

On original body. K * R 114

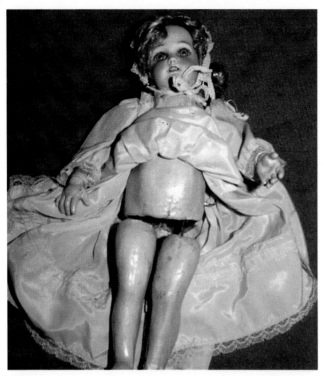

Walking mechanism body, bisque head, paperweight eyes

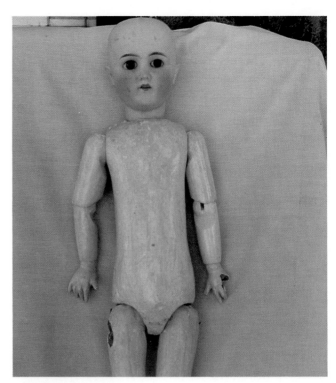

Kestner body, B6 head

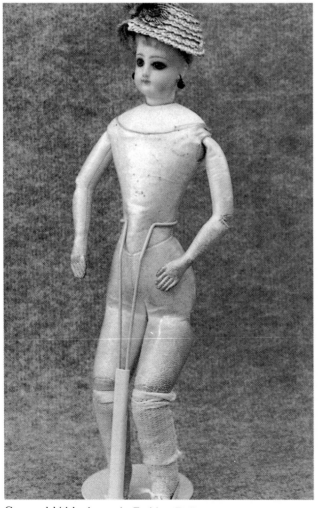

Gusseted kid body, early Fashion Doll.

Straight kid body, early Fashion Doll.

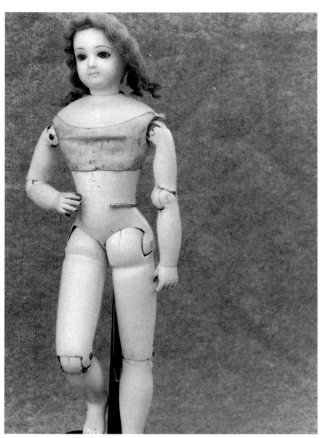

Blown kid body, Jumeau head. Madame Clement Fashion Doll. *Author's collection*

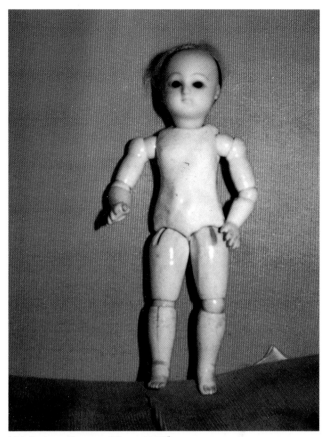

'A' Steiner France, 27 cm (10½")

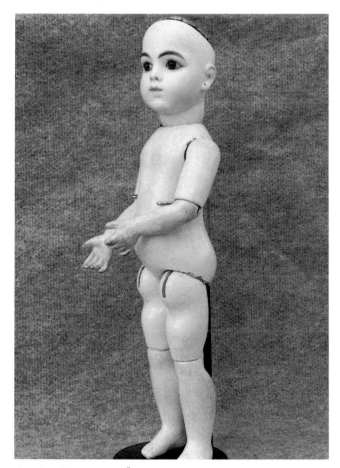

Bru Jne 7. 41 cm (16")

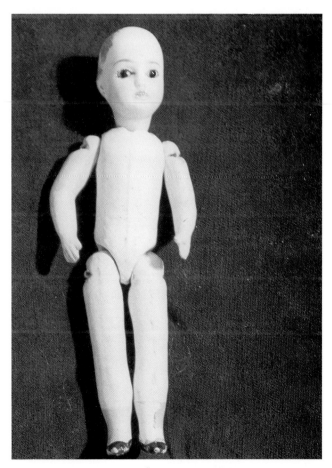

Limoges, France, 20 cm (8"). *Kempsey, NSW*

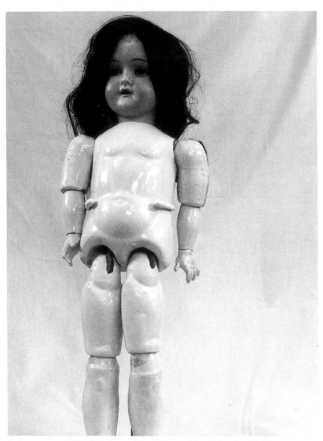

Schoenau & Hoffmeister head on original body with
Schoenau & Hoffmeister marking

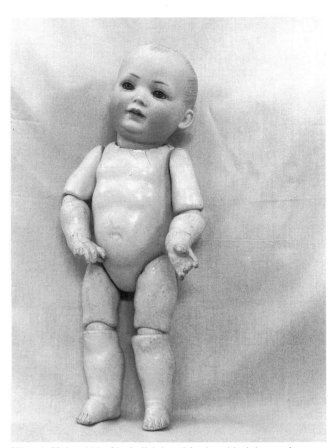

Kley & Hahn 532. Six ball jointed body, side joint on legs.
Author's collection

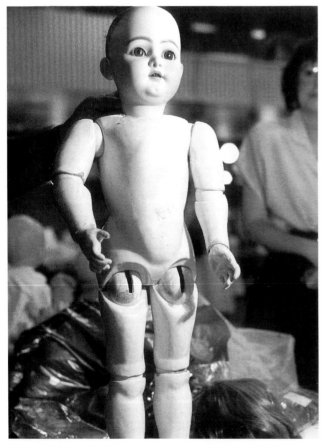

On original marked F. Schmidt body, 1893 mark. Six ball
body, extra balls at shoulders. *Private collection, Kempsey NSW*

Unusual body—all original—has extra papier mâché
shoulderplate over composition body. Hole at side is for
Mama, Papa strings used by Herman Wegner. *Kempsey NSW*

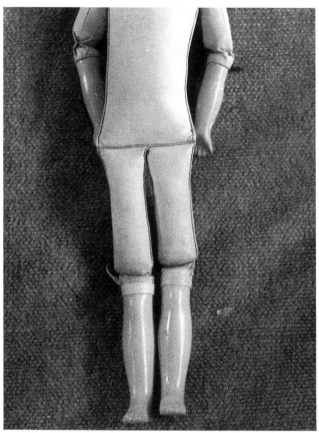

First World War Kidlyn body on English doll, Hancock head. *Taree NSW*

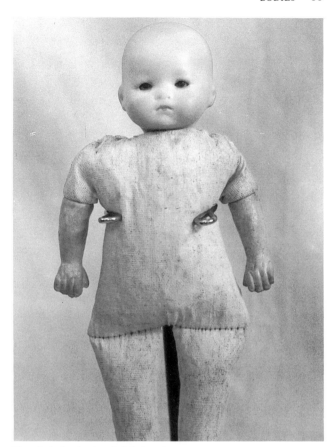

Simple baby body, A.M. head

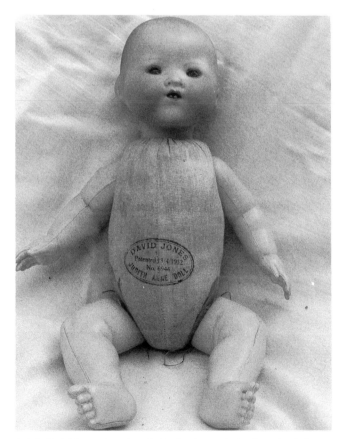

A.M. 351 bisque head on baby body made by Laurie Cohen (Sydney) for David Jones, Sydney. Doll marked Judith Anne, 1934–35

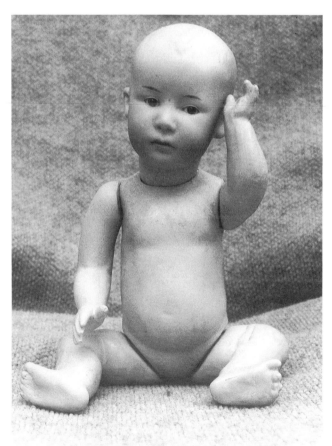

Gbr. Heubach, 76002
Composition baby body. *Toowoomba, Queensland*

SFBJ 301
Body marked on back Tete Jumeau

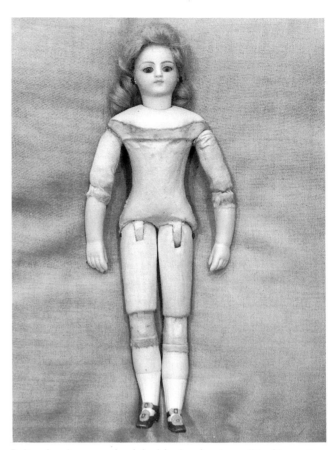

Belton head, unusual original body—head possibly Simon & Halbig. *Private collection, Tasmania*

A.M. 390
28 cm (11″). *Discovery Corner, Brisbane*

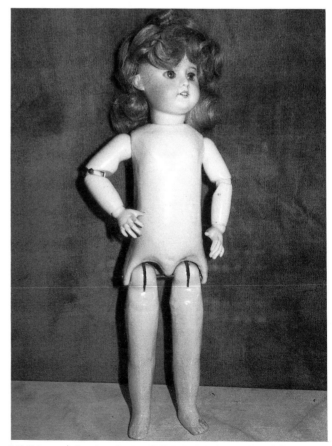

Walking mechanism body, S.F.B.J. Kissing doll. Right arm moves as though throwing a kiss

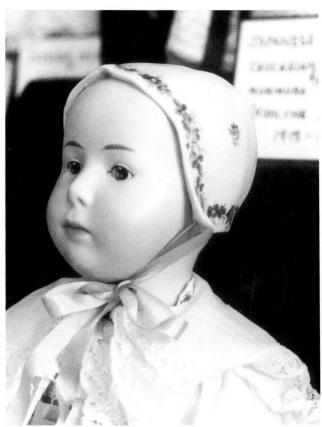

Bonnet head Stuart Baby by Gbr. Heubach, showing decoration on bonnet. This is the intaglio eye version. *Private collection, Sydney*

Bonnet head Stuart Baby by Gbr. Heubach, sleeping glass eye version. Notice the difference in bonnet decoration. *Private collection, Sydney*

In the early 1880s Adolf Wislizenus of Walterhausen took a doll to Thuringia from the factory of Emile Jumeau, France. Wislizenus was probably the first Thuringian doll factory owner to reproduce these ball jointed bodies. The early ball jointed doll bodies of Walterhausen had eight individual balls and were very similar to their French prototypes, however they are easily recognisable as German made because of their unsightly upper thighs. J. D. Kestner (Walterhausen) introduced Excelsior doll bodies in 1892 and because of the beautiful modelling in these ball jointed bodies, they conquered the markets worldwide. Kammer & Reinhardt developed new upper thighs obviating the joints twisting and turning. Heinrich Handwerck also was one of the pioneers who brought the ball jointed body to perfection.

Bonnet Head
This term refers to a bisque doll that has a shaped bonnet as an integral part of the head. A prime example of this type is the famous Stuart Baby by Gebr. Heubach.

Bonnie Babe 1928–30s
Bisque headed baby doll designed by Georgene Averill and distributed by Geo. Borgfeldt. The bisque heads were made in Germany by Alt, Beck & Gottschalck. There were only two sizes made at first, but the doll proved so popular that six sizes were soon made as well as one of all bisque. The smaller bisque headed dolls had a cloth body with celluloid hands, whereas the larger sizes had cloth bodies and composition arms and legs.

It is possible that J.D. Kestner also made some heads for this doll.

Bonnet head. Moulded hat, hair and shoulderplate. *Ulverstone, Tasmania*

Borgfeldt, George & Co. New York, USA

George Borgfeldt was a distribution company established in 1881 to import French and German dolls into the United States. The firm was also responsible for commissioning Grace Storey Putnam's Bye-lo baby doll and Rose O'Neill's Kewpie, two of the most successful dolls ever made. Borgfeldt also had contracts with German companies to make dolls' heads especially for them, such as the character baby by Armand Marseille in 1913 that bears both the G.B. trademark of Borgfeldt and the A.M. of Armand Marseille. Mould numbers used were 327, 328, 329. Dolls with the G.B. mark are occasionally found in Australia.

British National Dolls Ltd (B.N.D.) London, England

Before September 1933 the firm was situated at Cricklewood, London. They shifted to 4–8 Hutton Grove, Finchley, London and by 1942 were at Acton Lane, Harlesdon, London.

In 1933 they made dolls with china heads — what is now referred to as painted or sprayed bisque.

1934 Manufactured a new born baby doll Sunshine Babs and character dolls with wigs. Another doll with a painted bisque head called Chubby was referred to by the firm as the 'wonder doll' of 1934. All dolls were on composition bodies.

Bru Jne & Cie Paris and Montreuil-sous-Bois, France 1866–99

Leon Casimir Bru who founded the firm Bru, started his career with a lady doll that had a bisque head with separate shoulderplate on a full leather body. The bisque head was most likely produced at that time by Gaultier.

By 1869 the Bru company could offer the lady doll in these variations:

1. Complete leather body, including arms and hands
2. Leather body, jointed arms and hands made of wood or hard rubber
3. Body fully jointed, made of wood, hard rubber or even gutta percha.

After the death of Leon Casimir Bru, Mrs Appolene Bru managed the company until Casimir Bru took charge.

The Bébé revolution did not go unnoticed by Casimir Bru, but he was unable to decide whether to produce jointed bodies out of papier mâché or leather. His leather bodies were made in proportion of 1:5 that is five times the height of the head (without neck). So began the Circle Dot Bru, whose body was stuffed with cork shavings and horsehair for a lighter, better body. In October 1879 Bru patented the Bébé Téteur, which was a doll-child that when supplied with a bottle could drink. These dolls had the leather body of the Circle Dot Bru, but from 1883 had the so-called 'Cheviot' body, and from 1890 a jointed body of either wood or composition.

Casimir Bru sold the firm to Henri Cheviot in 1883, but the firm continued to use the name Bru and became Bru Jne. Cheviot designed a new body which is the one coveted and admired by collectors today. The kid body has bisque arms (sometimes even wooden) that are not rigid but jointed to the upper arm. The lower leg is made of wood and is jointed to the thighs. He also used a jointed composition and wood body with a well defined waist.

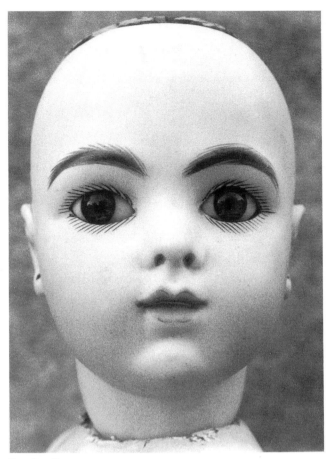

Bru Jne 7
Composition and wood body. *Author's collection*

Bru Brevette, kid body. *Lesley Hurford collection*

Bonnie Babe (Georgene Averill). Head by Alt, Beck & Gottschalck

The Bébé Bru could at last stand. Proportion was also changed with the doll now having a well defined waist. These changes made the Bébé Bru a very successful doll, but the Bru company never produced the large numbers of dolls that Emile Jumeau did.

In 1890 Paul Girard, a relative of Casimir Bru, became the new head of the House of Bru, and his most important patent was the Bébé Petit Pas.

The Bébé Petit Pas was registered on 23 September 1891. The doll has a large brass clockwork mechanism in the composition jointed body. The head moves from side to side and the legs move back and forth when the mechanism is wound. Some also have a Mama–Papa voicebox as part of their mechanism.

Bru dolls are known for their beautiful paperweight eyes, pierced ears and open/closed mouths, and they usually have cork pates.

The following is a short summary of the company:

Bru Jne R-11
Bébé Petit Pas, walker. *Baddow House, Maryborough, Queensland*

Circle Dot markings ⊙
Leon Casimir Bru	1867–70 ⎫	Fashion and Lady dolls
Mrs Appolene Bru	1870 ⎬	Bébé Brevette
Casimir Bru	to 1883 ⎭	Bébé Téteur

Bru Jne BRU JNE
Henri Cheviot	1883–89	Fashion and Lady dolls
		Bébé Téteur

Bru Jne R. BRU. JNE R 11
Paul Girard	1890–99	Bébé Téteur
		Bébé Petit Pas

In 1899 Bru joined with other French manufacturers to form the firm S.F.B.J. (Société Française de Fabrication des Bébés et Jouets). Curiously the mark 'Bébé Bru' was renewed in 1938 and 1953 by S.F.B.J. This is why some dolls marked Bru Jne have a closed painted mouth, and are in the style of the 1930s and 1940s type of dolls.

Burggrub Baby see Schoenau & Hoffmeister, Germany
A lovely character baby with a bisque head and composition bent limbed body. The markings on the bisque socket head denote that the head was made in the Porzellanfabrik Burggrub—the porcelain manufacturing company owned by Schoenau and Hoffmeister in Burggrub.

Burggrub Baby by Arthur Schoenau

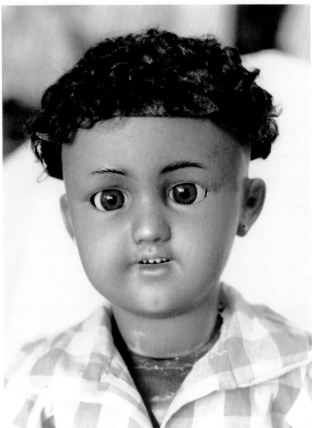

Brown 1278, Simon & Halbig, Germany, S & H 9. *Private collection, Queensland*

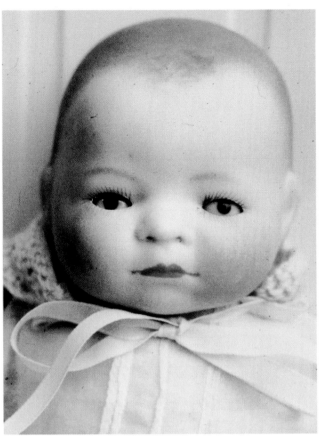

Bye-Lo Baby by Grace Story Putnam. *Dorothy Boland collection*

Character doll Porzellanfabrik Burggrub, Princes Elizabeth/5/Made in Germany. *Private collection, Queensland*

Bye-Lo Baby 1922

Design by Grace Storey Putnam, USA, the Bye-Lo baby was copyrighted in 1922. The design represented a three day old baby. By 1925 this popular doll, often referred to as 'The Million Dollar Baby', was made in 7 sizes ranging from 9″ (23 cm) to 20″ (51 cm). The cloth bodies for the flange version were made by K & K Toys, New York and were made in the curved leg ('frog') version or with straight legs, and had composition or celluloid hands.

© 1923 by
Grace S. Putnam
MADE IN GERMANY

The bisque heads (with sleeping eyes) were supplied by various German manufacturers such as C.F. Kling & Co., J.D. Kestner, Hertel Schwab & Co., and Alt, Beck & Gottschalck whose mould numbers 1372 (flange neck) and 1369 (socket head) were used. An all bisque version was made by J.D. Kestner. George Borgfeldt was the exclusive distributor for the American market.

Catterfelder Puppenfabrik Catterfeld, Germany, 1906 + , doll factory

Catterfelder
Puppenfabrik   C P

1906 Advertised 'stiff-joined small dolls, ball-jointed dolls, bisque shoulderplates and socket heads', including head with mould number 264 manufactured by J.D. Kestner.
1909 Mould number 206 registered.
1910 Registered trademark 'C.P.' Character child dolls with mould numbers 207 and 219. Character babies marked 200 (with domed head, painted eyes, similar to

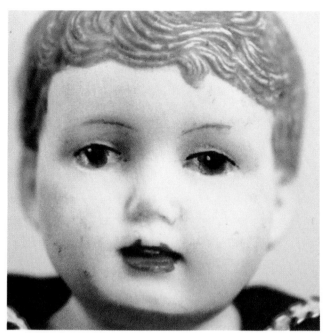

D.P.C.—England
Shoulderplate, painted eyes, moulded hair

Catterfelder Puppenfabrik. Mould 0½

K * R 100 mould), 201, 208, 209, 262, 263, also some of these moulds were produced in black.

1912 Babies with moveable tongue, mohair and fur wigs.

1919 Specialised in ball jointed dolls, bent limb and jointed babies, with and without hair style, dolls' heads and baby heads, hairstyled and unhairstyled bisque heads.

The mould numbers in their 200 range of dolls referred to character dolls, whereas their moulds 1100, 1200 and 1357 were ball jointed dolls.

C.C., Limoges, France see *Chauviere & Cie*, Paris

Character dolls

Before the turn of the century, most dolls' heads were manufactured with simple planes to their faces and heads. This type of countenance is referred to by collectors as a 'dolly face'. These 'dolly faces', because of the ease of release from their moulds, cleaning, etc., were mass produced over the years and are the type of heads that are most commonly found. Examples of the so-called 'dolly face' are the 390 and 370 moulds of Armand Marseille, and the 1079 mould of Simon & Halbig. The fact that they were mass produced and therefore relatively easy to find even today, in no way detracts from the beauty found in many of these dolls.

At the beginning of this century, dollmaking firms, particularly those in Germany, were looking for something different to sell to their customers, and a more life-like baby proved to be the answer. Kammer & Reinhardt with their mould 100, and other German manufacturers (including Theodor Recknagel with the New Born Babe) had perfected these babies and were ready to manufacture them when the onset of World War I slowed down and then stopped production until the war ended.

The 1920s were the hey-day of character dolls with both French and German firms perfecting this type. The numerous baby dolls of the 1920s and the excellent child dolls of K * R and S.F.B.J. are beautiful examples of the character dolls which are now so eagerly sought by collectors.

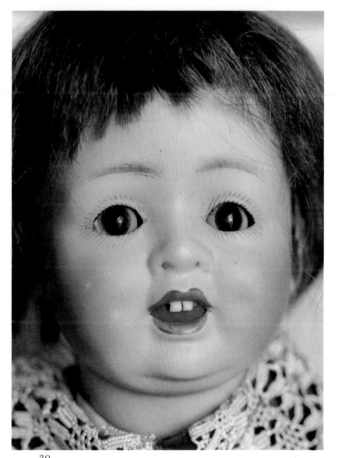

30
CP (Catterfelder Puppenfabrik)

C.C. Limoges (Chauviere & Cie)

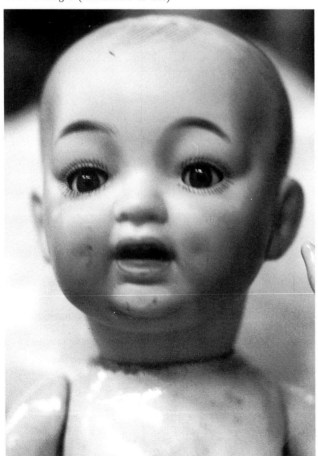

Character Baby, manufacturer unknown

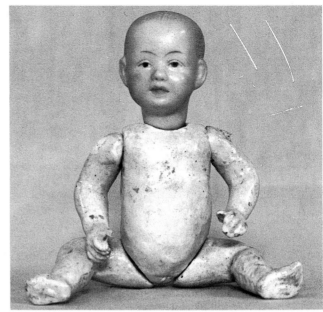

206 (C.P)

Chauviere & Cie Paris 1870–90

C.C.
LIMOGES
FRANCE

1863–77 Mlle Chauviere appeared in Paris directories
    under the heading 'Dolls'.
1890 Was listed as specialising in jointed dolls.

Clement, Pierre Victor Paris 1866–75
1867 Issued with a French patent for making dolls entirely
    of embossed leather.
Later advertised that he made a light strong and finely
jointed doll in natural leather. Dolls under this category can
be found with various French heads ranging from Bru to
Jumeau and Rohmer. The doll body is finely moulded to
a lady shape, light and very mobile. These dolls are
presumed to have been handled by Madame Clement, and
are now referred to by her name.

Clement, Vve (widow) Paris 1870s
This firm is known to have handled dolls, presumably with
the beautiful bodies of 'blown leather' made by Pierre
Clement, that can be found with different bisque 'lady'
heads by famous French manufacturers. These Lady or
Fashion dolls are referred to as 'Madame Clement' dolls.

Clothing
Throughout this book, where possible, I have used photographs of dolls showing their original clothing or costume.
Many collectors do not like the simple clothing old dolls are
found in, take off these old clothes (often throwing them
away) and redress their dolls in over elaborate pretty clothes,
trying to emulate clothes they may have seen in a book.
It must be remembered that not all dolls were originally sold
in pretty and over elaborate clothes. Many came to Australia
undressed or just clad in very plain muslin type chemises.
Australia was a long journey by ship from the sources of

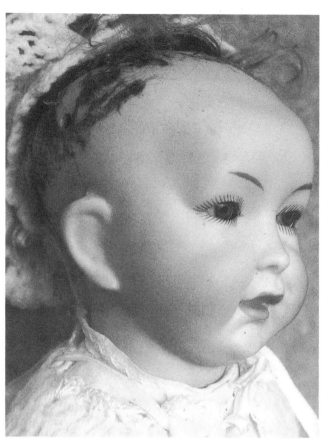

Character Baby. Note high crown and high cut for pate, manufacturer unknown. Mark B/2/Germany

Madame Clement, France. Blown leather body, Jumeau bisque head (swivel head). *Author's collection*

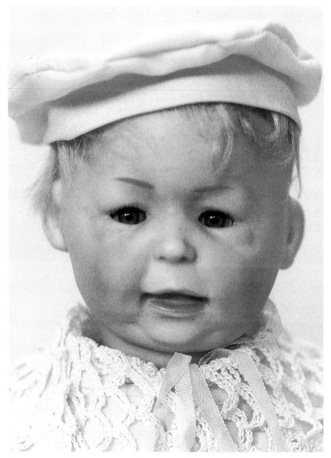

Character child, maker unknown. *Private collection, Queensland*

French character doll, mark S.F.B.J./235/Paris. *Private collection, Queensland*

Original clothes from an 'RE' NIPPON. All commercially made 1915–22. Note the simple chemise

dolls in France and Germany, and these dolls came to Australia in the holds of sailing ships last century and took over six weeks by cargo vessel this century. Every bit of cargo space was precious, so dolls were packed as closely as possible into large crates, to get the maximum amount of dolls in every shipment. In some countries customs duty was assessed by weight in earlier years rather than by quantity, so the least a doll weighed the better.

When the dolls arrived at the wholesalers or import firms, they would often be dressed by specially employed women at large stores such as David Jones and Myers, in dresses that would suit the stores' clientele. Other dolls would be sold in their simple chemises for mother, aunt or grand-mother to dress for a little girl. Thus it is important to keep all old doll clothing, whether it be commercially made or homemade, as long as it looks as though it was specially made for the doll, in the doll's era.

Commercially made clothes of the period of the doll add to its value, and should always be kept with the doll even if it is redressed by another owner. To keep such original clothes in the condition you received them, they should be stored in acid-free tissue paper.

Should the doll be without clothes when you get it, carefully study as many photographs or dolls at doll fairs, etc. as you can, and then make new clothes out of material that simulates that of yesteryear, cottons, silks, etc.; definitely not nylon or nylon lace for anything before the 1950s.

Fully original K and K doll, USA. Bisque china shoulderplate head marked K & K Germany. *Lesley Hurford collection*

1248 Simon & Halbig. The dress was pale blue silk with an embroidered medallion at the front partly covered by bretelles

Fully boned corset that was on a Fashion doll

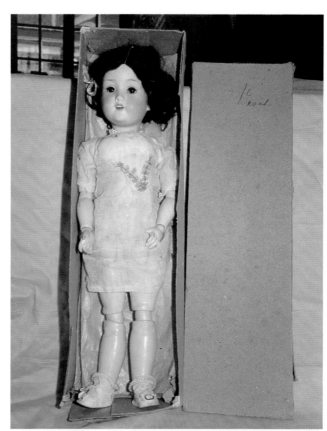

Armand Marseille 390 in original chemise, shoes and socks. The boxes were often made or assembled here

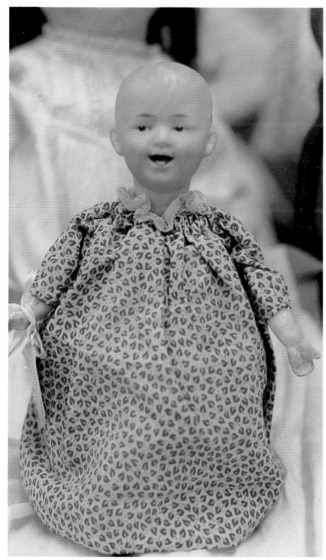

Mechanical walker. Gbr. Heubach. *Courtesy J. Brooks, Quaint Collectables*

Dream Baby 341   *Tamworth*

J.D. Kestner, 13.235, shoulderplate. *Sydney*

Simple original clothing on dolls that have been passed down through families, mark A.M. 390

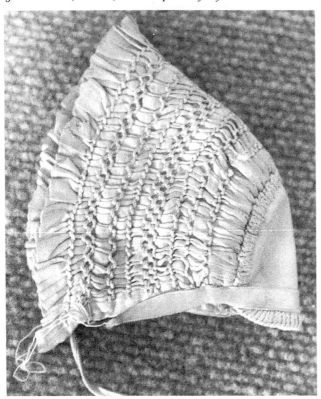

Smocked hat from Gebr. Knock doll 185 18/0

S&H in original Norwegian costume, mark 1078/Simon & Halbig/S&H/6½. *Private collection, Brisbane*

Blue silk, smocked at yoke, mark Gbr. Knock 185 18/0. *Ipswich, Queensland*

Fully original clothing on a Laurie Cohen Hush-a-Bye doll with German bisque head marked A.M. 382. *Private collection, Gulgong NSW*

C.O.D. Cuno & Otto Dressel see Dressel, Cuno & Otto, Germany

Cohen, Laurie Sydney, Australia 1930s–50s, wholesaler and doll factory

Laurie Cohen wanted to produce a good quality bisque headed doll at a reasonable price, so he imported bisque heads, mainly flange necked baby heads, from Armand Marseille of Koppelsdorf, Germany. He then had cloth bodies made in his workrooms to the design he registered in 1932. To these bodies he fitted celluloid arms and legs that he imported from Japan. The dolls had a shield shaped trademark with L.C. and Hush-a-bye printed on the front of their bodies. The dolls were sold dressed and undressed throughout Australia, except when World War II stopped the importation of the necessary materials. The most common mould numbers found on these dolls are 341, 351, 352, 382 and 384 by A.M.

Damerval Freres & Laffranchy Montreuil-sous-Bois, France 1910?–16

Jules and Charles Damerval were the owners of the company Damerval Freres (Bros) & Laffranchy who are thought to have manufactured dolls with the markings Montreuil Bois France and the initials D. L. found on the bisque heads of dolls.

The majority of bisque heads found with these markings represent men, some even have moulded moustaches, but dolly faced dolls with rather pointed teeth were also apparently made with these markings. The doll shown in the photograph bearing the inscription as described is over 45 cm (18″) tall, and would be regarded as having a dolly face.

Danel & Cie Montreuil-sous-Bois, France 1889–95, factory

1889 Danel and Cie registered Paris Bébé and a picture of the Eiffel Tower as their trademark in France. These are found on dolls' bodies.

1891 Registered in France the trademark Bébé Français.

1892 Specialised in negro and mulatto dolls, a very early French reference for this type of doll.

E 5 D
DEP
FRANCE

Danel of Danel & Cie was at one time a director of Jumeau; his partner M. Guepratti was formerly in charge of making glass eyes for Jumeau.

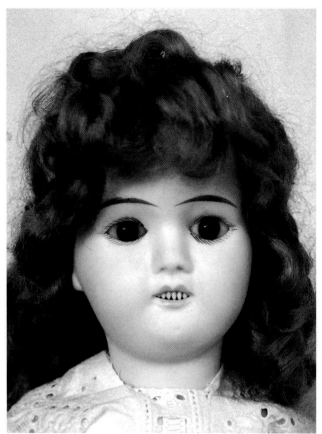

Damerval Freres & Laffranchy, France. *Private collection, Brisbane*

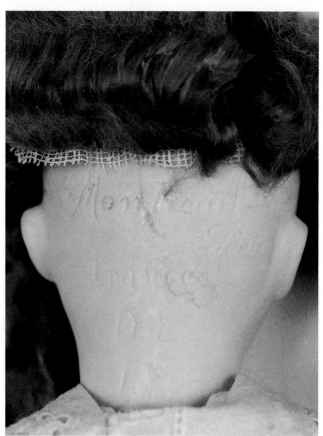

Back view showing marks. Damerval Freres & Laffranchy, France

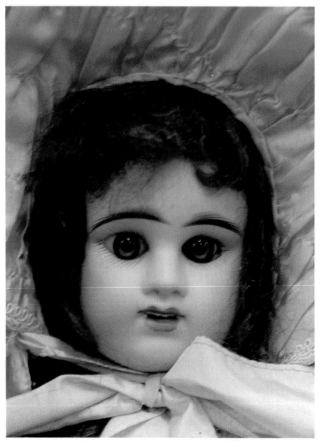

E.D
Danel & Cie. *Courtesy Jacki Brooks, Quaint Collectables*

Demalcol Catterfeld, Neustadt & London 1921–24
The name 'Demalcol' was derived from using parts of the distributor's name in London, DEnnis MALley & CO. of London.

Demalcol
5/0
Germany

They advertised baby dolls, jointed dolls and also undressed dolls. The 'Demalcol' trademark can also be found on a Googly type bisque doll's head. Dennis Malley & Co. were the originators of the Dainty May, Little Sunshine and May Blossom Dolls. The bisque heads on these dolls are attributed to Catterfelder Puppenfabrik.

DEP
These markings basically mean that the doll's head design has been registered in either France of Germany. It is an abbreviation of the following: Deponirit (Dep)—markings used on German dolls claiming registration; and Déposé (Dep)—markings on French dolls claiming registration. Because both France and Germany have used this abbreviation it is sometimes hard to define the actual origin of a doll's head, especially when it only has the letters DEP or dep on the back of the head.
To add to the confusion, German dollmakers made dolls' heads for French firms. One example of this practice was Simon & Halbig who made bisque heads bearing DEP for the firm Fleischmann & Bloedel (a German firm that was

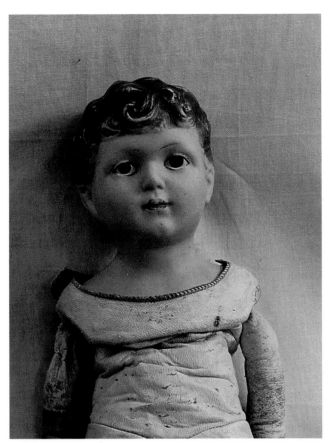

D.P.C.
Doll Pottery Co., England

D.P.C., England
123-9

also based in France) for sale on the French market. Jumeau was a notable French firm that used German heads, possibly by Simon & Halbig, and such heads with DEP are sometimes found on composition ball jointed bodies that are marked Jumeau, and also on S.F.B.J. bodies.

Other manufacturers used the word dep or DEP on their bisque heads.

Doll Pottery Co. Fenton, Stoke-on-Trent, England 1915–22, factory, dolls heads, etc.

On 16 April 1915 the company registered as a manufacturer of dolls' heads and limbs. This company produced possibly the greatest variety of dolls and dolls' heads in England in numerous sizes during the period of operation. Many of their better class heads were made from classic designs by well known artists of the day and special models were also made to customers' own designs. Each model was made in five or six head sizes.

New models in April 1917 included Pierots, black dolls and clowns.

In February 1920 they advertised a range of fully jointed dolls in three sizes, one of which had the trademark Cecily. There were also girl and boy babies, three models of which

All bisque, dolls'-house doll on couch from dolls' house, 1900–10. *Hervey Bay, Queensland*

Dolls'-house dolls

French costume on French composition body, unmarked head

could have fixed glass or sleeping eyes. The firm closed its doll production in April 1922, being unable to compete with the influx of bisque headed dolls from Germany.

Note: This company is sometimes confused with the Diamond Pottery Co. also of Stoke-on-Trent, who are thought to have manufactured dolls during World War I, but not enough evidence has been found to thoroughly support the suggestion.

Dolls'-house dolls 1890–1920 +

Small all bisque dolls, or bisque heads on cloth bodies (usually 6″ [15 cm] or smaller) which were made by various German firms. These dolls were made to people dolls, houses, that were so popular as toys late last century and early this century.

Many of these small dolls have painted moulded hair, painted eyes and simple bodies of cloth. Other dolls'-house dolls were made with moveable pocelain limbs fixed to a one piece body and head. Some even had tiny sleeping eyes. They were made to represent all the people needed to populate a dolls' house, such as female servants, cooks, nannies, butler, coachman or chauffeur, fathers, mothers, children, etc.

Dolls in national or ethnic costume

Often small bisque headed dolls can be found wearing national or ethnic costume of various countries around the world.

In this type of doll, the authenticity of the original costume is as important as the origin of the bisque head on the doll. The small dolls used, often have no marking whatsoever on their bisque heads, or else marks of doll factories that very little is known about.

Unfortunately, over the years it has been the custom of many doll collectors to undress these small ambassadors, throw away what they consider tatty or not-so-pretty clothes and redress them, thus losing their originality.

Strictly speaking, these small tourist dolls of yesterday are fashion dolls. They reflect the costume and customs of a country or region during a certain era of history. Most of these dolls were souvenirs from other countries brought to Australia by travellers, many of them returning World War I soldiers. Special doll factories in Germany offered up to one hundred different costumes. During the 1920s and 1930s Unis France dolls were used for this purpose.

Dressel, Cuno & Otto Sonneberg, Germany, 1870 + , factory and Verlag house (agency for small factories and home industries)

The firm of Dressel is acknowledged as the oldest doll making company for which records exist, originating in 1789. The company made its own dolls as well as buying bisque heads from Simon & Halbig, Armand Marseille and Gebr. Heubach.

Unknown, Germany, closed mouth

Two S.F.B.J. bisque headed dolls in French provincial costume. *Private collection, Sydney*

Moulded hair, blonde bisque, Scottish costume

Moulded hair, blonde bisque, Norwegian costume. *Courtesy, N. Theodore, Tamworth NSW*

Schoenau & Hoffmeister 1000, Germany

Shoulderplate, mark 6/0XX A.M C.O.D. 93-C DEP made in Germany

Helmet mark COD. *Ulverstone, Tasmania*

C.O.D. Jutta. *Courtesy J. Brooks, Australian Doll Digest*

1873 Registered the name Cuno & Otto Dressel.

1880 Displayed dolls at the Exhibition in Melbourne.

1888 Displayed dolls of every description at Exhibition in Melbourne.

1892 Bisque headed doll—mould mark C.O.D. 93—was supplied by Armand Marseille in sizes 0-10.

1898 Dressed dolls representing President McKinley, Admiral Sampson, Admiral Dewey and Uncle Sam, all in their respective uniforms with portrait porcelain heads by Simon & Halbig.

1907 Registered JUTTA PUPPEN trademark.

1910 c. Character Baby marked C.O.D. or Jutta.

1916 Advertised jointed dolls and babies marked Jutta.

1926 Advertised Jutta dolls—double jointed, toddlers and bent limb babies. Also advertised Rock-a-Bye Baby.

Used bisque heads from the following factories:

Armand Marseille—mould numbers 1776, 1893, 1896, 1898 (shoulderplates)

Simon & Halbig—mould numbers 1348 and 1349 Jutta; 1468 and 1469 Flapper dolls; 1848, 1849, 1912, 1914, 1920 Jutta

Ernst. Heubach—mould number 1922 Jutta

Gebr. Heubach—Character dolls

Also offered cheaper quality dolls depicting American

Indians and Eskimos to the United States market, most of which were unmarked as to origin, and were produced by numerous factories in and around Sonneberg.

C ☉ D 93·5 DEP.

D.R.G.M. Deutsches Reichsgebrauchsmuster
The initials D.R.G.M. mean German design patent, the legislation for which was enacted on 1 October 1891. It was the so called 'little patent' and protected an item which, under certain circumstances, could consist of many small inventions. Many dolls were marked D.R.G.M. and often the mark gave a hint to the registration number, which meant that the doll included an important novelty applied to it by the dollmaker.

Dump heads/tip dolls
These are doll pieces and dolls' heads that have been dug out of old dumps or dolls made from such pieces. These bisque pieces are usually recovered by people digging for old bottles. The heads found may be socket or shoulderplate and are often found damaged (particularly the shoulder of the shoulderplate version). This damage may have been the reason for them being in the dump in the first place.
The products of these diggings are a great source for the tiny bisque arms and legs needed for replacements on small all bisque dolls. Because of the chemicals in the ground and the other objects that were buried in the dump, leaching of colour and staining (particularly of a black or reddish colour) are common to dump finds.
When buying loose heads or limbs look for this staining or lack of colour, cracks or touch ups, etc. as these parts may have come from a dump. On the plus side—dumps often disgorge interesting and otherwise unprocurable pieces. It is up to you, the collector, to decide whether you buy or pass by.

Eden Bébé 1890–1925 +

EDEN-BÉBÉ

This trademark was registered in France and Germany by Fleischmann & Bloedel (Sonneberg and Paris) and by their successor S.F.B.J. for a line of Bébés.

*EDEN BEBE
PARIS
7
DÉPOSÉ*

These bisque headed dolls on composition bodies were made in the German factory of Fleishmann & Bloedel at Sonneberg. They were distributed in the United States in 1917 by Grey and Grey Ltd. Mark—EDEN BEBE PARIS
A kissing, walking flirty eyed doll with a 1039 Simon & Halbig bisque head bore the Eden Bébé label in 1892.

E.H. or E.H.K. see Heinrich, Ernst
E.I.H. see Horsman, E.I.

EDEN BEBE
Fleischmann & Bloedel. *Ulverstone, Tasmania*

EINCO Googly, head manufactured by Gbr. Heubach for Eisenmann & Co.

EINCO, Germany, Eisenmann & Co. *Private collection, Brisbane*

EINCO see Eisenmann & Co.
E.J. see Jumeau, Emile

Ellar c. 1925
Name found on a bisque baby head with oriental colouring, painted hair, closed mouth and glass eyes. The heads were made by Armand Marseille in both flange and socket head versions for cloth or composition bodies.

Eisenmann & Co. Furth, Germany and London, England 1881–1925 +, export business for dolls and toys
1881 Founded business for export of toys.
1895 Altered trademark to include dolls.

Einco
0
Germany

The trademark Einco can be found on bisque baby socket heads with painted dome heads, painted eyes, closed or open/closed mouths on bent limb baby bodies. A socket head with googly eyes was made for Eisenmann & Co. by Gebr. Heubach—mould number 8764 with both firms' markings.

English Bisque
During World War I many English firms, particularly the pottery companies in Stoke-on-Trent and London areas, stepped in to make dolls and dolls' heads for home consumption. Many of the pottery companies used a poor grade clay rather than the fine kaolin used for bisque heads. Thus many English heads, although described as bisque, are actually pottery heads.

The majority of these English made bisque heads are much more florid in colour and have a coarser, grainier finish than those made in Germany and France.
Because of this fact, here in Australia these often second grade heads are not overly popular with collectors; but if you are collecting a range of bisque headed dolls, one of these dolls is a must for your collection.
There was a considerable list of makers of this type of doll, but some of the best were made by the following manufacturers:

British Doll Manufacturing Co. 1914 + —Character dolls
Doll Pottery Co. Ltd 1915 +
W.H. Goss & Co., Stoke-on-Trent 1917 +
S. Hancock & Son, Cauldon, Staffordshire
Laurie Hanson & Co., London
Hewitt & Leadbeater, Stoke-on-Trent, Willow Dolls
Mayer & Sharrat, used Melba and M & S England as marks
Nunn & Smead 1915–1927, Nunsuch dolls
Messrs Speight, Classic Works, Dewsbury, Yorkshire 1917 +, china headed dolls with fully jointed Kidette body

Most of these firms ceased manufacture of dolls' heads in 1922 as they were unable to compete with the dolls coming from Germany at that time. Nunn & Smead continued until 1927, and then in the 1930s the firm of British National Dolls made porcelain heads with a sprayed finish that were equal to the same type of doll from Germany during the depression years.

Erste Steinbacher Porzellanfabrik (First Steinbach Porcelain Factory) Steinbach
1900 Founded by Max Kieswetta, who was a sculptor.
1912 Hugo Wiefel bought the company, becoming Wiefel & Co.
1914 Dolls' heads were advertised.
1923 Robert Carl and son-in-law Gustav Heubach were silent partners. New name of firm Erste Steinbacher Porzellanfabrik Wiefel & Co. Was again manufacturing bisque heads.
1930 Produced bisque dolls' heads. Owners were still Gustav Heubach and Robert Carl.
1936 Robert Carl died.
1937 Gustav Heubach listed as sole owner and the firm was still producing bisque dolls' heads—painted and sprayed.
Mark EStP in a stylised oval shape.

EStP
Germany
23

EStP see Erste Steinbacher Porzellanfabrik
E.U.ST. see Steiner, Edmund Ulrich

Eyebrows
In the early days of the manufacture of bisque dolls' heads, all heads had been moulded without eyebrow profile. Later many innovations were tried to achieve a more natural type of eyebrow. The inserted eyebrow of fur found in Floradora bisque heads by Armand Marseille is just one of these inventions. The finely feathered eyebrows found on some dolls are quite remarkable when compared to the simple straight line of other heads.

It must be remembered that some bisque heads had 'transfer' eyebrows. These were commercially printed artificial eyebrows that were applied before the final fire, and fired onto the head.

In 1892 the moulding of eyebrows as part of the bisque head was begun with a design patented by F. & W. Goebel, Germany.

Eyelashes

On many of the bisque heads of last century and early this century, the only eyelash adornment was the eyelashes that were painted around the eye area before the final kiln fire. Many dolls' heads manufactured by S.F.B.J. have straight eyelashes painted on the bottom eyelid area only.

Separate eyelashes for dolls were first introduced by Simon & Halbig in 1893. Further ideas for separate eyelashes using hair, thread or even feathers were tried, attaching them in various ways to the glass eyes or lids. A method of attaching lashes to the underside of the separate eyelids that were used on flirting eyes proved to be quite effective in giving a realistic look.

Eyes

From the inception of the first bisque heads for dolls in the middle of the 19th century, many and varied types of eyes were used to give a more life-like appearance to the otherwise inanimate objects. Some of the types of eyes used were:

Painted eyes China headed dolls generally had painted eyes, but from the 1860s and 1870s bisque dolls' heads were fitted with inserted or stationary eyes. When character dolls, such as K * R's mould 100 were first created in 1909, dolls eyes were again painted, as it was found to be almost technically impossible to insert stationary or sleeping eyes in this type of doll. This rather flat style of painted eyes was overtaken after 1911 by the invention of conically deepened eye sockets in the unfired porcelain, now referred to as intaglio eyes.

Stationary eyes The early glass eyes of the 19th century were black or brown in colour with no pupil. By the middle of the century these stationary or set-in glass eyes had improved immensely, with beautifully threaded iris eyes found in German dolls, and the extraordinary depth of the paperweight eyes used in many of the French Fashion dolls and French Bébé dolls.

Sleeping eyes The first tip-up or sleeping eyes were achieved by pulling threads or wire to open and close the eyes. Many inventions followed, some of which were quite weird, until the ones most commonly seen now were achieved. These consist of two spherical glass eyes joined by a bridge of special material with a weight suspended from the middle of the bridge by means of a wire. When the doll is held upright the weight points to the floor. The weight swings to the back of the head when the doll is in a horizontal position. The two holes often found in the back of bisque dolls' heads were where the eye weight was tied during transportation.

Intaglio eyes Sometimes referred to as hollow eyes. These painted eyes are deeply recessed and moulded into the porcelain head before firing. This type of eye is found mainly

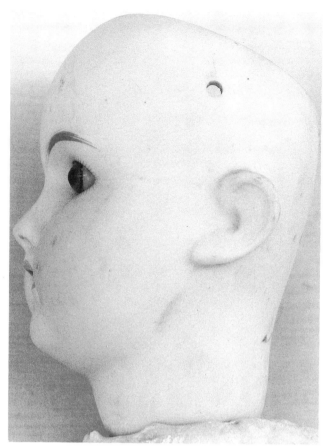

Side on view of Kestner B6 set-in eyes (non sleeping)

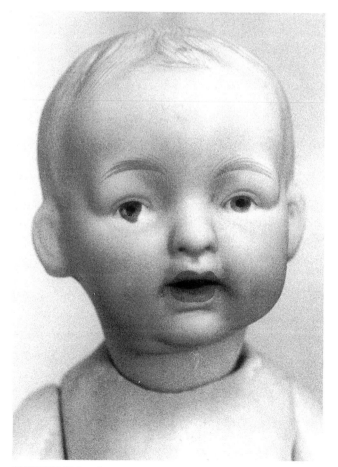

NIPPON Painted eyes

Gbr. Heubach, intaglio eyes, 7684. *Courtesy Jacki Brooks, Australian Doll Digest*

on character dolls, and one firm, Gebruder Heubach, specialised in them. The effect of these painted eyes is a deep, quite natural expression.

Googly eyes Also called roguish eyes, these are exaggerated eyes, usually of glass, and are placed to the side of the eye socket. This type of eye was probably stimulated by the large round eyes found on early Kewpie dolls. In 1912 many different doll factories applied for patents.

Flirting eyes This type of glass eye was not only able to sleep, but was able to look from side to side, depending on how the head was held. First invented by Otto Gans in 1901, the mechanism for these eyes was often delicately balanced from a thread hanging at the inside front of the forehead.

Exhibitions in Australia 1879, 1880, 1888
In the latter half of the 19th century Exhibitions or Expositions were held at least every year (often twice) at locations where firms could show their wares, such as Paris, Amsterdam, Liverpool, London, Barcelona, Brussels, Porte Alegre (Brazil), Cinncinatti and Chicago, as well as three that were held in Australia. Most of these Exhibitions or Expositions had dolls as part of their various exhibits. The following awards were won by doll companies at the three Australian exhibitions.

1879 Sydney

First Degree Merit	France	Jumeau
Highly Commended	France	Villard & Weill
	Germany	Fischer, Naumann & Co.
Commended	Germany	Lambert & Sammhammer
		Moschmann & Huffner
		Rock & Graner

1880 Melbourne

Gold Medal	France	Jumeau (dolls, Bébés)
Silver Medal	France	Bru (dolls, Bébés); Falck
Bronze Metal	France	Jumeau (mechanical; Lejeune; Vichy
	Germany	Fischer, Naumann & Co.; Unger, Schneider & Co. (mechanical)
Certificate	France	Bru (mechanical); Martin; Potiers
	Germany	Wagner

Jumeau Fashion doll, paperweight eyes

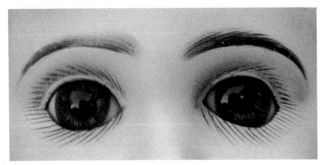

Tete Jumeau S.D.G.D.
Paperweight eyes, eyelashes and eyebrows

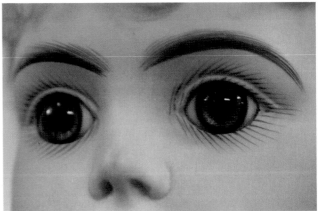

Bru Jne R
Eyebrows, eyelashes and paperweight eyes.

No Award   Germany   Dorst; C. & O. Dressel; Fleischman Bros; R. Heinze; J.C. Lindner; L. Lindner & Son; Muller & Strassburger

Japan   T. Hayashi; Kiriu Kosho-kuwaisha; T. Akiyama

Australia   P. Thomle (mechanical)

1888 Melbourne

Gold Medal	France	Bru; Vichy
Silver Medal	Austria	Frankl
	France	Falck & Roussel
Award Unknown	France	Bru (Cheviot)
	Germany	Max Oscar Arnold; Cuno & Otto Dressel; Heubach; Kampfe & Sontag; P. Recknagel

Many of the names are well known, others have faded into obscurity; and not all awards would have been for bisque headed dolls.

Fashion or Lady dolls 1860s-70s

Due to the fact that most of the early bisque dolls' heads were unmarked or marked with only a letter or number indicating size, the origins of many of the fine Lady or Fashion dolls of the 1860s and 1870s remain a mystery. Among the makers that are known to have made heads are Gaultier, Bru, Jumeau, Huret and Rohmer.

These dolls were often very elaborately costumed in the latest Paris fashions. Some were even sold with small travelling trunks complete with extra clothes and accessories, such as miniature purses, fans and even parasols. Because of the mode of dressing these dolls, they became known as Fashion dolls or even Parisiennes.

The heads used in these dolls were shoulderplate swivel heads with closed mouths, pierced ears, glass paperweight eyes or painted eyes. Bodies found on these dolls can be all kid—gussetted or ungussetted, cloth or kid over a wooden jointed body, an uncovered well jointed wooden body or even a jointed body of finely blown leather.

F.G. see Gaultier, François
F.I.B. see Bierschenck, Fritz

Flange necked bisque head

This type of head is more commonly found on baby dolls that have cloth bodies. It refers to a bisque head that has a circular lip or groove in the base of the neck, allowing the cloth body to be wired or tied to secure it to the head.

Fleischmann & Bloedel Furth, Sonneberg, Germany and Paris, France 1873-1926, factory for toys and dolls

1873 The company was founded.
1890 Eden Bébé registered as a trademark for all doll products.
1895 Manufactured a talking doll.
1896 Doll that walked automatically by means of driving wheels in feet, body of composition with the head manufactured by Simon & Halbig.
1898 Registered Bébé Triomphe for dolls.

F.G. shoulderplate, kid body, French fashion

All original Jumeau fashion, 10½″ (26.5 cm). Unusual in that it represents a teenage girl, 1870-1880s.

French Fashion, original clothes

Spare set of clothes and hat, French Fashion

French fashion showing detail of back of costume. Jumeau head

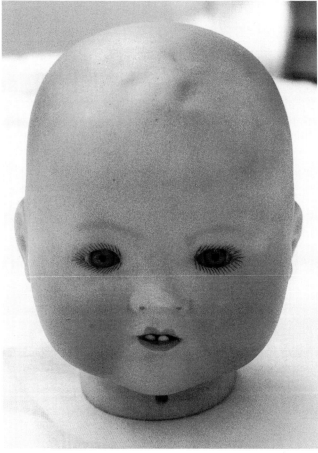

Flange neck, bisque baby head A.M. 351, Dream Baby

1899 One of the founder members of S.F.B.J. in co-operation with eight other French companies. Fleischmann became a director.

1914 Fleischmann gave up his directorship of S.F.B.J. with the onset of World War I.

Fleischmann & Bloedel was the first company to re-establish contacts with France after the war of 1870-71. At first France was hesitant, but soon Fleischmann & Bloedel were the main exporters of toys and dolls to France. Because of the declining demand for toys in the French toy industry in 1899, eight companies including Fleischmann & Bloedel combined to make one big concern to try to stave off the onslaughts of the very progressive German doll industry.

Eden-Bébé

On the advice of Fleischmann, S.F.B.J. and other doll factories like Jumeau purchased bisque doll heads produced in Thuringia. Fleischmann also took original Jumeau moulds to Thuringian factories to have them manufactured there, later to be assembled as dolls in Paris.

DEP
70

French manufacturers of bisque heads

Although much is written about the beauty of French dolls, substantial research leads one to believe there were only a few actual French manufacturers of bisque dolls' heads. These include the well known names of Bru, Danel & Cie, Gaultier, Jumeau, Pintoul & Godchaux, Jules Steiner and later the conglomerate S.F.B.J.

F.S. or **F.S. & Co.** see Schmidt, Franz

Fulper Pottery Co. Flemington, New York, USA 1918-21, factory

The manufacture of bisque dolls' heads by the Fulper Pottery Co. began in 1918 with the firm of Horsman & Co. assisting in the production. The first report of this company in June 1919 listed two baby head dolls and two girl dolls, all produced in two sizes.
By 1920 the firm was producing a range of eight socket baby heads, ten socket girl heads and six shoulderplate heads and

these were being produced to fit dolls ranging in size from 13″ (33 cm) to 22″ (56 cm). A few of their bisque dolls' heads have moulded hair and intaglio eyes. Dolls of all bisque were also produced. Some of their heads are marked with either Horsman or Amberg in conjunction with the Fulper mark.

Gans & Seyfarth Walterhausen, Germany 1908-22, doll factory

G & S 6
Germany

1908 The factory was founded and dolls were made with moveable eyes. Registered patents for eye mechanisms, including flirty eyes in 1910, 1912, 1913, 1914, 1916, 1919.
1921 Advertised that they made jointed dolls, toddlers and bent limb babies. Took out patents for googly and flirting eyes.

Gans & Seyfarth
126
Germany

1922 The two factory owners parted. Otto Gans opened his own factory; Seyfarth registered under the name Seyfarth & Reinhardt.

Gaultier, François (Gauthier prior to 1875) St Maur, France 1860-99

F. G

François Gaultier made porcelain dolls' heads and doll parts for Lady dolls and Bébés which were sold to many of the French makers of dolls.
1872 He took out a French patent for a method of cutting out and inserting glass eyes into bisque dolls' heads.

1875 Changed name to François Gaultier (from Gauthier).
1881 The porcelain used for making heads was still in the form of paste, and not slip.
1885 Became Gaultier Freres (Gaultier Bros).
1899 Became part of the S.F.B.J. conglomerate, receiving one hundred shares. His contribution was material and products.
Bisque heads with paperweight eyes, closed mouth and pierced ears, bearing the trademark F.G. (after becoming Freres Gaultier in 1885) may be found as swivel headed shoulderplates on gussetted kid bodies, lower bisque arms, or as socket heads on ball jointed bodies.

G.B. see Borgfeldt, George

Gebruder or **Gbr.**
Gebruder is German for brothers and is found in conjunction with names such as Gbr. Heubach, Gbr. Kuhnlenz and Gbr. Knock.

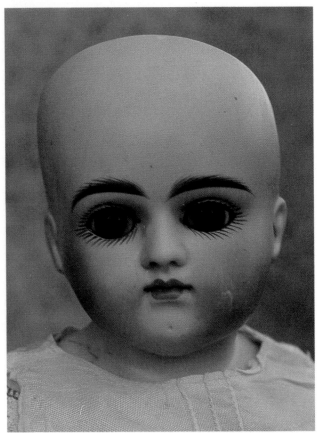

Shoulderplate, Kestner?

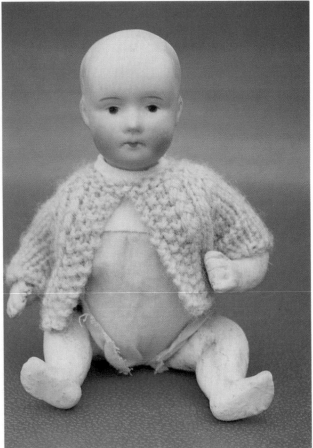

Bisque head, composition baby body. Maker unknown, mark
P.3. *Doll & Toy Collection, Brisbane*

German bisque heads manufacturer unknown
There are many, many bisque dolls that as yet cannot be positively identified, both as to the manufacturer and the doll factory where they were made. Some of these dolls are unusual, of beautiful or very poor bisque, but all remain an enigma. Many have marks, initials, numerals or no identification at all.

Gesland Paris, France 1860-1928, doll factory
The firm of Gesland made, exported, distributed and repaired dolls.
In 1881 bisque heads were purchased from François Gaultier.

E GESLAND
B^TE S. G. D. G.
PARIS

During World War I and later Gesland used Petite Française bisque heads by J. Verlingue on their dolls.
The name Gesland is now more commonly used in conjunction with a type of doll body. The name has been found on stuffed bodies with a wire frame covered with stockinet. These were used on Fashion dolls, often with F.G. marked heads.
Besides these dolls they marketed dressed and undressed Bébés with bisque heads in a range of eleven sizes from 13″ (33 cm) to 31″ (79 cm), as well as selling separate bisque heads.
In 1921 the firm advertised that the dolls they sold were made entirely in France.

G.H. see Heubach, Gebruder
G.K. see Kuhnlenz, Gebruder
G.K.N. see Knoch, Gebruder

Goebel F. & W. Oeslau, Germany 1879 + , porcelain factory
A porcelain factory that made excellent dolls' heads, half dolls and bathing beauties in both bisque and china.

1879 Started production.
1887 Were producing twelve types of porcelain socket heads, some of which had moulded hairstyles.
1892 Doll head with modelled and profiled eyebrows.
1893 Produced 129 different models of shoulderheads, socket heads and straight heads. Some models were made in up to 21 sizes.
1908 Produced baby dolls and bathing dolls.
1921 Between 1921 and 1932 many new dolls' heads were sculpted by W. Moller, R. Unger and K. Simon.
1924 Produced tea cosy heads, doll heads, bathing beauties and harem beauties and also dolls similar to Kewpies.

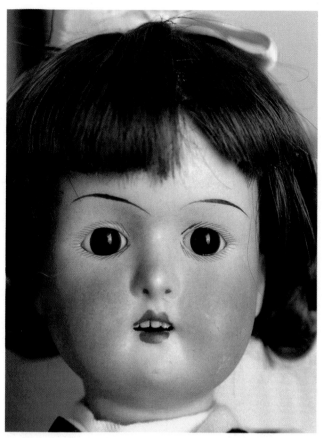

F. Goebel, crown over WG/120/2/OX

Goebel Googlies. *Lesley Hurford collection*

Produced heads for Max Handwerck, with the early half moon mark after 1910. Mould numbers were 217, 283, 285, 286 Bébé Elite.

The company used two marks.

Early mark—triangle, half moon and 2 digit number.

From 1900, a crown and the initials W.G. intertwined.

Googly or doll with **roguish eyes**

The dolls under this category have eyes, often exaggerated in size, that are fixed or moving so that they glance or move to one side. These types of eyes were painted or made of glass and gave the doll a comical, normally happy look. Due to their popularity early this century, many doll firms made these dolls, including:

Bahr & Proschild mould no. 686; Gebr. Heubach 'Einco' mould no. 9566 and others; Kammer & Reinhardt mould no. 131; Kestner mould nos 189, 221, 165; Simon & Halbig; S.F.B.J. mould no. 245; Herm. Steiner; Recknagel; Goebel; Armand Marseille mould nos 200, 210, 240, 241, 252, 253, 254, 255, 258, 310, 323, 324, 325; Hertel & Schwab for Strobel & Wilkin mould nos 163, 165, 172, 173; Demalcol; Kley & Hahn mould no. 189; and Fulper Pottery, USA.

Goss, W.H. & Co. Stroke-on-Trent, England, porcelain factory

W.H. Goss & Co. produced dolls' limbs and dolls' heads with painted and glass eyes. Their bisque heads, which are now considered rare, were rather crude and highly coloured when compared with the bisque heads by German and

All bisque painted eye Googly, 13 cm (5"). *Private collection, Queensland*

Gbr. Heubach Googly. *Courtesy J. Brookes, Quaint Collectables, Goulburn NSW*

Japanese painted eye Googly, composition body. *Courtesy Doll & Toy Collection, Brisbane*

All bisque Googly, 13 cm (5"). *Private collection, Queensland*

Googly by Recknagel. *Courtesy J. Brooks, Quaint Collectables, Goulburn NSW*

Mark 35 in 6 pointed star, Nippon. *Private collection, Taree*

Mark. Star/300H/Nippon W/S/M.*Private collection, Brisbane*

French makers, but because of their rarity command good prices today.

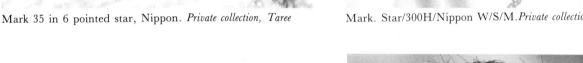

GOSS
30

During World War I Goss & Co. were encouraged to produce substitute heads to make up for the part Germany had taken in dollmaking. The modelling of the heads was good and suggests that they could have been based on German dolls' heads, but the quality and decoration were poor in comparison.

The firm produced child dolls in 1914 with shoulderplate heads, wigs, inset or sleeping glass eyes and closed mouths with lips painted dark red, on a cloth body. A character baby was produced c. 1918 with flanged head, painted hair and eyes, open/closed mouth painted dark red and a cloth body. By 1917 they were producing jointed and unjointed dolls from 11″ (28 cm) to 30″ (76 cm) with glass and painted eyes. They also produced bisque heads for the English firm Potteries Toy Co. Although the dolls were expensive, they were beginning to capture the English market when Germany again went into production making cheaper prettier dolls.

The firm was taken over by Cauldon Potteries in 1934 and became Goss China Co. Ltd. In 1940 they were producing baby dolls with flange china heads and in 1941 they were making heads modelled by craftsmen from photographs.

Greiner & Co. Steinbeck, Germany, doll factory
Mainly a maker of leather dolls and leather bodies for heads

Bisque head, glass eyes, composition body. Japan. *Private collection, Tasmania*

All bisque Pixy toy, Japan, squeaker in cut out in stomach.
Grannys, Brisbane

C. Kling, all original. Shoulderplate marked 168

All bisque, Japan

which were purchased from Armand Marseille, Ernst. Heubach and Christian Eichhorn & Sohn. Most of the finished dolls were sent to the American firm of George Borgfeldt.

G.S. see Gans & Seyfarth

Halbig, Carl Grafenhain, partner in Simon & Halbig.

HALBIG
K ✡ R
Germany

The mark Halbig only, in conjunction with K * R is not common, therefore, a doll bearing just Halbig, the letters K * R (Kammer & Reinhardt) and numerals denoting the finished size of the doll in centimetres is unusual and was probably made before the First World War.

For further information on the firms of Kammer & Reinhardt and Simon & Halbig look up their respective listings in this book.

Half dolls

Known also as pin-cushion or tea-cosy dolls. Most of these small doll-like objects representing the human form (normally a lady) from the waist up are modelled with a glazed china finish. Some German companies like F. & W.

1079 Halbig, S&H, Germany, 11½

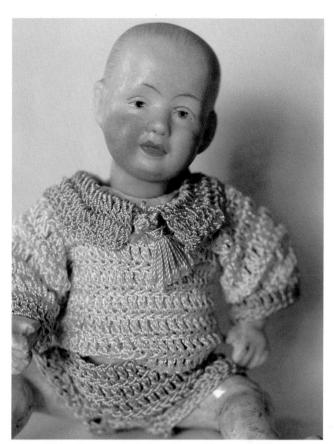

Catterfelder Puppenfabrik (?), 18 cm (7″), mark 206-2

Half doll, maker unknown. Moulded hair, moveable arms.
Ulverstone, Tasmania

Half doll by F. & W. Goebel

Hancock, England, shoulderplate. *Taree NSW*

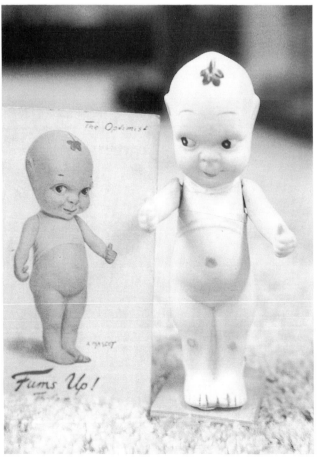

Fums Up, Hancock & Son, England, with Fums Up postcard. *Lesley Hurford collection*

Goebel made lovely bisque half dolls, often with their arms extended away from the body in delightful poses. These exquisite heads, which have a great deal of detail in their moulded costume, can be found atop powder bowls, handkerchief sachets and tea cosies.

Hancock & Son Cauldon, England
Soon after the start of World War I Hancock & Son were commissioned by Hamleys, London to produce Fumsup, a china mascot, and afterwards a series of rather similar dolls with moving arms called Lulu, Wuwu and Eyes Right.

With prompting by the Board of Trade, it was only a short step to regular production of dolls' heads and limbs. By 1917 the firm was making 70 varieties of bisque heads, some with moulded hair, with other open pates for wigs. Their heads were made with open or closed mouths, with painted eyes and also with glass eyes that the firm manufactured themselves. The bisque of their heads was similar to that used by other English firms, highly coloured and porous, and they were unable to compete when Germany came back into production. They made specialised lines for other English doll assembly firms.

Handwerck, Heinrich Walterhausen, Germany 1886–1930, doll factory

1886 Heinrich Handwerck made leather doll bodies in white calf and also pink cloth bodies. To these bodies were added shoulderplate heads and wigs, and the dolls were then dressed in simple shifts and shipped to the world under the Handwerck trademark.

The firm was told by their United States agents to dress their dolls to look more like French dolls and to label the cardboard doll boxes in French.

Little is known about early Heinrich Handwerck production, but dolls with shoulderplate bisque heads marked with what is thought to be an early mark, HcH in conjunction with a horseshoe, are found in Australia.

It is known that Simon & Halbig supplied bisque dolls' heads to Heinrich Handwerck following Handwerck's designs. Some of the mould numbers supplied by Simon & Halbig are: 69, 79, 89, 99, 109, 119 (shoulderplates); 139, 199 (socket heads); some 79 and 89 models had closed mouths.

1888 Around this date the firms of Heinrich Handwerck and Kammer & Reinhardt were rivals.
1898 Registered the trademarks for dolls Bébé de Réclame and Bébé Cosmopolite, both ball jointed dolls.
1901 Heinrich Handwerck had so many orders from overseas that there was doubt that the factory would be able to meet the demand.

1902 Heinrich Handwerck died and Kammer & Reinhardt purchased the factory, allowing it to continue under Handwerck's name.

1910 Advertised that they were a factory producing fine ball jointed dolls, also spare heads, wigs and their speciality, character dolls.

1918 The firm was closed by Kammer & Reinhardt.

1921 Heinrich Handwerck Jnr returned from the USA and reopened the Handwerck factory which was then situated at Gotha. Registered trademarks for dolls, doll heads, doll bodies, joints, dresses and wigs.

1923 A large amount of pre World War I dolls were sold in Latin America.

1932 The firm was declared bankrupt.

Handwerck, Max Walterhausen, Germany 1900–30, doll factory

The firm of Max Handwerck made dolls and doll bodies. He had many of his own designs produced as bisque heads by William Goebel. These dolls' heads were socket or shoulderplate heads and bore the early Goebel trademark, the half crescent moon.

His most successful range of dolls was known as Bébé Elite. They were bisque character headed dolls with sculpted hats as part of the heads, in various forms representing personalities of World War I. Many of these dolls had googly eyes.

1900 The firm of Handwerck was incorporated.

Heinrich Handwerck, original clothes, 46 cm (18″), mark Hch H with a horseshoe

Happifat girl, all bisque, complete with part sticker. *Author's collection*

Max Handwerck, Germany, 3½, 66 cm (26″)

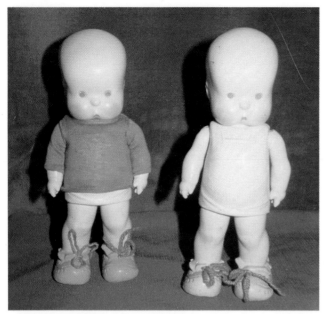

HEbee and SHEbee. 24 cm (9½")

Shoulderplate kid body, circa 1915. 38 cm (15"), mark
Germany/275-12/0 Heubach Koppelsdorf

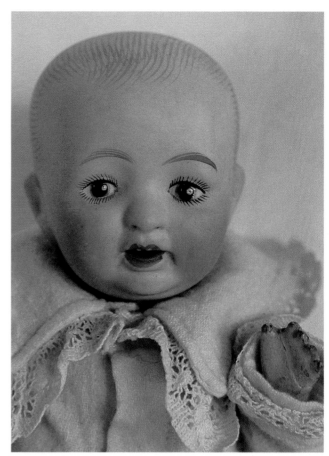

Painted eyes that have been glazed to give them more life.
Hertel, Schwab & Co. Mould no. 3/3/0 *Private collection,
Brisbane*

1901 Registered the name Bébé Elite.
1902 Handwerck died, and his wife took over. Advertised
      Triumph Bébés, ball jointed dolls that could walk, sit,
      stand and move head and arms in natural movements
      while walking.
1922 Advertised Bébé Elite and 'The Handwerck Cele-
      brated Doll'.

Happifat Germany and Japan 1913-21
These delightful small all bisque character dolls were
registered in the USA by Geo. Borgfeldt. Designed by Kate
Jordan, they were produced in a male and female version.
The rotund boy is dressed in an outfit of green tailed coat
and fawn trousers, the girl in moulded dress of pinkish
lavender and both have unusual moulded and painted hair.

HEbee and SHEbee 1925-27

Based on illustrations of Charles Twelvetrees, these bisque
character dolls were registered in the USA by E.I. Horsman.
The 9" (23 cm) all bisque versions of this character doll have
a one piece head and torso with moulded chemise painted
white. The dolls were jointed at the shoulders and hips with
moulded shoes, blue for HEbee and pink for SHEbee,
through which were laced separate shoelaces.

Hertel, Schwab & Co. Mould no. 3/151. *Betty Brown collection*

Hertel, Schwab & Co. Glass sleeping eyes, composition body, 23 cm (9″), mould no. 3-2/0. *Author's collection*

A small verison of this doll in a whitish bisque was available for sale in Australia in the 1970s. The doll bore a paper label with 'Shackman—Made in Japan'.

Hertel, Schwab & Co. Stutzhaus, Germany 1910-30 + , porcelain factory

36/3
Made
in
Germany

The firm was founded in 1910 by three sculptors—August Hertel, Heinrich Schwab, Friedrich Muller—and Hugo Rosenbusch, a porcelain painter. Until recently many of the character bisque heads produced by Hertel, Schwab & Co. have been erroneously attributed to the firm of J.D. Kestner. The character heads of Hertel, Schwab & Co. were made of a fine bright bisque in two variations:

Domed head, eyes painted in blue with closed or open mouth. Mould numbers include 130, 142, 150, 151, 152, 125.

Socket heads, wigged, sleeping eyes of grey/blue glass, open mouth, moulded or moving tongue. Mould numbers include 134, 149, 141.

Also all bisque dolls were produced with jointed arms and legs, mould number 208. Most bisque dolls' heads were marked with a series number, size number and sometimes 'Made in Germany'.

The company also exclusively produced special number series bisque dolls for the American market including the Bye-Lo Baby for George Borgfeldt and Jubilee-Doll, a series with googly eyes for Strobel & Wilkin. Hertel, Schwab & Co. supplied bisque heads to the factories of Kley and Hahn, Koenig & Wernicke (mould numbers 98, 99, 157 and 176), Rudolf Walch etc.

1920 Made bisque doll heads, character heads, babies, character dolls, bathing dolls and employed one hundred workers.

1930 Their production included bisque heads, doll heads, baby heads, porcelain dolls, tea cosy shoulderheads, pin cushions.

Heubach, Ernst Koppelsdorf, Germany 1887-1932 + , porcelain factory

1887 Founded a factory with the manufacture of porcelain slip as one of its activities. Later in year opened a porcelain factory.

Heubach Koppelsdorf
320·○○
Germany

1888 Finest bisque doll heads and bathing dolls advertised. During the early years of production the firm produced mainly shoulderplate bisque heads marked with a horseshoe. Mould numbers 1900, 1901, 1902, 1906, 1909.

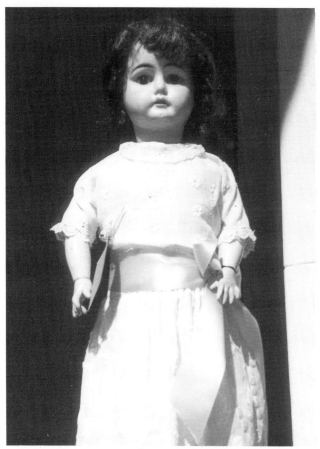

Original clothes, 51 cm (20″), Heubach Koppeldorf 900–0

48 cm (19″), Heubach Koppelsdorf 250–2/0

Shoulderplate kid body, circa 1915. 38 cm (15″), mark
Germany/275–12/0 Heubach Koppelsdorf

Mark Heubach Koppeldorf/300–2/Germany. *Private collection
Brisbane*

1910 c. Specialised in producing character heads including Blacks and Mulattos. Character bisque baby heads were also produced, mould numbers 300, 320, 342.

Moulded hair, painted eyes Googly dolls were produced in bisque in the following mould numbers: 260, 261, 263, 264.

1919 Ernst Heubach and Armand Marseille merged and became Vereinigte Koppelsdorfer Porzellanfabrik (United Porcelain Factory of Koppelsdorf).

1932 Ernst Heubach and Armand Marseille separated and became two separate establishments.

Ernst Heubach produced bisque dolls' heads for A. Wislizenus, Seyfarth & Reinhardt, Gbr. Ohlhaver, Cuno & Otto Dressel and coloured heads (South Sea babies mould number 399) for A. Luge & Co.

Heubach, Gebruder Lichte, Germany, 1910–38, porcelain factory

1840 Brothers Christoph and Philipp Heubach purchased a porcelain factory.

1882 Registered the trademark of a 'rising sun' in conjunction with four figure numbers (mould numbers).

1887 After the death of the original owners, Philip and Ottaker Heubach became sole owners.

1910 First mention of the production of doll heads. Registration of the 'squared monogram' trademark.

1911 A patent issued for a doll head, presumed to be the typical Heubach head, with painted deepened eyes (intaglio). Participated in the Leipzig Fair where doll heads by Heubach were first introduced to the world.

Original clothes, mark Heubach Koppeldorf 320-2 Germany.

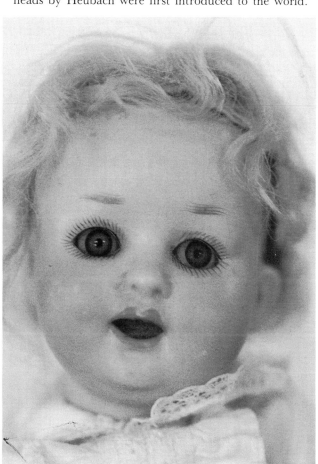

Mark Heubach-Koppeldorf/300. *Private collection, Brisbane*

Heubach Koppelsdorf, made in Germany. 'Horseshoe', dep D/O shoulder plate, cloth body. *Private collection, Brisbane*

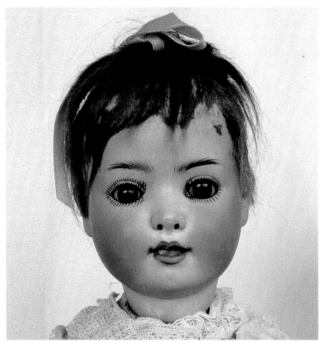

Open nostrils and moveable tongue, original hair Heubach Koppeldorf 321. *Private collection, Brisbane*

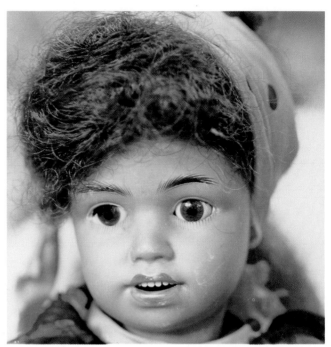

Ernst Heubach, shoulderplate, cloth body, mark Made in Germany 'horse shoe' dep D/O. *Private collection, Brisbane*

Original clothes mark Heubach Koppeldorf/321-0. *Private collection, Brisbane*

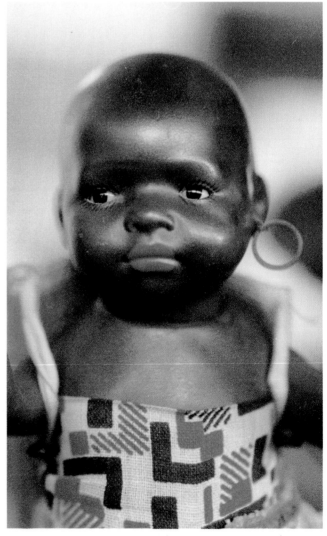

Mark Heubach Koppeldorf 399 10/0. *Private collection, Taree*

Produced character doll heads which were amusing and extraordinarily moulded with domed heads, painted moulded hair, intaglio eyes and closed mouth. Some of these heads are: Babies on bent limb composition body, head mould numbers 6894, 7602, 6898, 7759, 7604. Shoulderplate heads, pouty or smiling with intaglio eyes, mould numbers 10532, 10586, 10633. Stuart Baby (bonnet head) mould numbers 7877, 7977. The Screamer mould number 7684. A special characteristic of many Gbr. Heubach bisque heads is the pink bisque used to achieve a more natural skin colour. This coloured bisque has caused much consternation to many doll collectors who at first think they may have bought a reproduction doll.

1923 Art doll and tea cosy dolls were among those advertised.

Gbr. Heubach also made small all bisque dolls, whose mould numbers are often unreadable because of the heavy use to which these moulds were subjected. It must not be forgotten that Gbr. Heubach made 'piano' babies (or dolls as they are sometimes called)—beautifully moulded one piece bisque babies and young children, with or without wigs, usually in moulded white chemises with blue trim.

1938 Still offered porcelain dolls and bisque heads.

Went into bankruptcy. A friend tried to maintain the estate, but the company was closed.

During their years of operation Gbr. Heubach produced bisque heads for other companies: Otto Schamberger (Adlon), Hamburger & Co. (Dolly Dimple), Eisenmann (Einco), Gbr. Ohlhaver (Revalo, including Coquette 7788 for the United States market around 1912), Wagner & Zetsche (Whistling Jim), Cuno & Otto Dressel.

Gebr. Heubach 8192. *Private collection, Sydney*

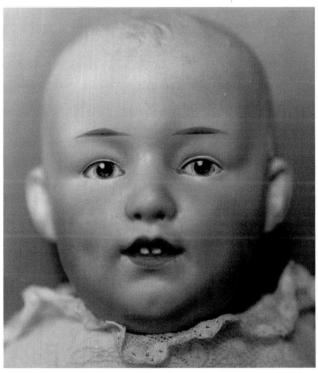

Gbr. Heubach, shoulderplate, mould no. 48/Germany/7854

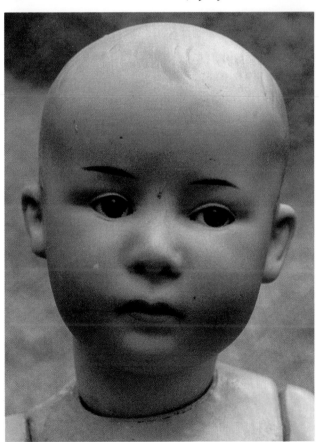

Gbr. Heubach, 76002. *Private collection, Toowoomba Queensland*

Gbr. Heubach, shoulderplate. *Private collection, Queensland*

Gbr. Heubach Character. *Lesley Hurford collection*

Gbr. Heubach Stuart Baby, painted eyes, original clothes, "press me and I'll cry" on band around waist. *Lesley Hurford collection*

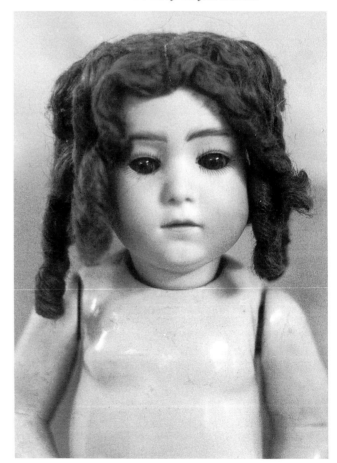

Gbr. Heubach. Glass eyes, pink bisque

Unknown doll on funny wooden body. See how neck is attached to block of wood. 9 cm (3½"). *Private collection, Brisbane*

Hewitt & Leadbeater (Hewitt Bros) Willow Pottery, Willow St, Longton, Stoke-on-Trent, Staffordshire, England 1907–26

WILLOW□ENGLAND

H & L
WILLOW◊ENGLAND

1907–19 the firm was known as Willow Pottery.
1919–26 known as Hewitt Bros.
Dolls' heads were made by Hewitt and Leadbeater from 1914. Their well equipped factory was the first to manufacture dolls' heads in England after the outbreak of World War I. So great was the demand that they had to take over another factory solely to produce doll heads and other component parts.
By 1917 they were producing thousands of shoulderheads, many with moulded hairdos and socket heads with painted eyes or prepared to take glass eyes. Many of the dolls' heads sported painted hair styles.
A trademark incorporating H & L and a willow tree symbol was used.
Hewitt Bros continued to make dolls' heads after 1920.

Hoffnungs Sydney, Australia and other States 1920–40s, wholesalers.
Australian wholesale firm who during the 1930s imported vast quantities of German manufactured bisque heads—

UA1V—Hush-a-bye Dolls, with china or composition heads, sleeping eyes, and voice; soft body, celluloid arms and legs. Nicely dressed in pretty Organdi Frock. Size, 14in., as illustrated. Special Value, 9/11. Larger sizes: 16in., 12/6; 18in., 16/11; 20in., 19/11.

Hush-a-bye by Laurie Cohen. From a 1936 Grace Bros (Sydney) advertisement.

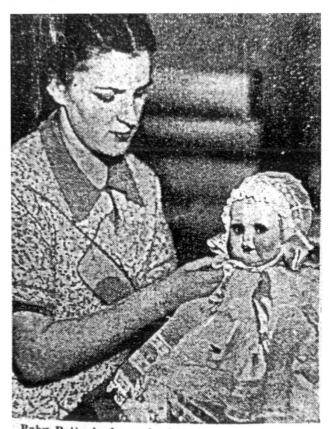

Baby Betty in her splendor
Thanks the handmaids who attend her.
But oh! her dark brown eyes are saying,
Why tarry, when we could be playing?

Hoffnung's. From an article in the *Australian Woman's Weekly* 4 September 1937 on 'Fascinating Dolls'. Taken in a doll factory where 1000 dolls a week were made

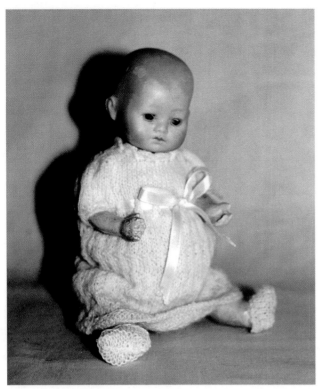

Tynie Babe ©. 1924 E.I. Horsman

particularly those of Armand Marseille. Both ball joined dolls and baby dolls were assembled in their small factory and workroom.

Bisque baby doll heads with flanged necks and celluloid limbs from Japan were attached to a specially designed torpedo shaped cloth body with gusset at crutch and no back seam (designed by Vera Kent) in their own workshop overseen by Vera Kent.

These and other assembled dolls were sold under the I-DOLL label.

Horsman, E.I. & Co. New York, USA 1878 + , distributors of French and German dolls

© 1924
E.I. Horsman Inc.
Made in
Germany

1893 Sold bisque head dolls with kid body, by Kestner; and also French Jumeau dolls. Sold doll parts and accessories including bisque doll heads. Japan made bisque heads for Horsman during or shortly after World War I, when German manufactured bisque dolls' heads were unavailable.

1920 Advertised bisque head dolls manufactured by Fulper USA.

1924 Tynie Babe, solid dome infant head in bisque, designed by Bernard Lipfert. It had sleeping eyes, closed mouth and was manufactured with a cloth body and composition arms or all composition body. This doll is also found in Australia.

A small all bisque version was made with a swivel neck.

1925 All bisque HEbee and SHEbee were made.

Hulss Adolf Walterhausen 1915–30 + , factory for dolls and babies

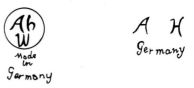

1925 Registered their trademark of AH over W, and this mark can be found in conjunction with Simon & Halbig on some bisque heads. These heads were manufactured by Simon & Halbig.

1926 Advertised that they made dolls of only highest quality, bent limb babies and toddlers, jointed dolls, dressed and undressed and spare parts.

Huret, Maison France 1812–30

BREVET DEP. s GDG
MAISON HURET   HURET
Boulivart Montmartre
PARIS

1850 Mlle Huret applied for a French patent for a moulded articulated dolls' body.

1851 Advertised all kinds of jointed dolls of a new type with porcelain heads.

1855 Mlle Huret exhibited articulated gutta percha dolls and the moulds used for their manufacture at the Paris Exposition, winning a Bronze Medal.

1867 Advertised that they produced bisque headed dolls, dressed dolls and showed dolls at the 1867 Paris Exhibition.

1868 It was reported that Huret made 1500 dolls a year. The dolls were dressed as ladies or children with astrakan fur or mohair for wigs, on heads of bisque, china, metal, gutta percha or wood. Made lady dolls with bisque heads and composition, kid, wood or gutta percha bodies, sometimes with metal hands and feet.

1890 Company now owned by Carette; advertised jointed Bébés and dolls.

1919–27 Again advertising dolls.

1927–30 + Made Bébés, and also advertised that they had porcelain heads.

Mark Huret or Maison Huret stamped on dolls' body.

Hush-a-Bye see also Cohen, L.C. Sydney, Australia 1930–40 +

Hush-a-Bye is the trademark used by Laurie Cohen, doll assembler (1930–40) of Sydney, Australia. This name can be found on torpedo shaped cloth bodies with front, back and side seams that have German bisque heads (particularly by Armand Marseille with mould numbers 341, 351, 352, 382 and 384) and strung arms and legs of celluloid from Japan.

A modern mass produced bisque shoulder doll head on cloth body

Painted bisque Red Indian

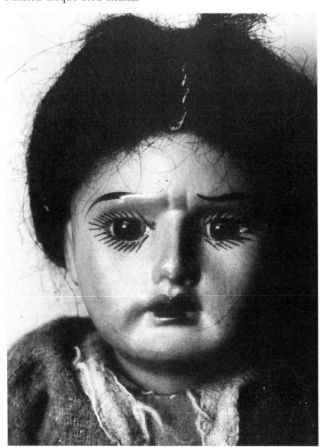

Red Indian doll's head, red brown in colour. Notice heavy brows. *Private collection, Tasmania*

The trademark incorporated a shield with L.C. and Hush-a-Bye within the shield. Often a girl's name such as Betty or Sally was also stamped on the body.

I-Doll

"I" Doll

Trade name used by Hoffnungs of Sydney, Australia, for many of the dolls that they assembled using parts from Germany (including bisque heads from Armand Marseille), the USA and Canada.

Indian dolls (American) with bisque heads

Dolls representing the Red Indians of the United States were manufactured by German firms for sale in the USA. Many were of a small size on quite simple bodies, dressed as squaws and braves. Some of these bisque headed dolls were made using standard heads painted a reddish brown colour with special emphasis around the eyes. Others came from moulds specially designed to imitate Red Indian facial features. Both Armand Marselle and Cuno & Otto Dressel manufactured these often cheap little dolls, and together dominated the market for this type of doll's head. Unfortunately few are marked with actual makers' marks, only numbers. These dolls are popular among collectors of ethnic dolls in Australia.

For the Canadians, Gbr. Heubach (mould numbers 9457 and 8457) and Simon & Halbig (1303) produced Eskimo type bisque heads and the dolls were dressed in fur or plush to represent the Eskimo costume. These dolls were part of the production of most doll factories.

Japanese bisque dolls Japan 1915–22 +

When German bisque dolls and dolls' heads were no longer available during World War I, Japan stepped into the breech, either copying or using German moulds. Firms based in the United States, such as Morimura and Yamato, had bisque heads made for them in Japan. Dolls bearing these two companies' marks were also sold in Australia. Other known marks on bisque heads with Japan or Nippon markings found in Australia are R E in a diamond, M in a stylised five-leafed shamrock, and A in a circle.

The bodies of these dolls, particularly on the shoulderplate head version, are mainly made of 'kidlyn' (an oiled cloth material). The socket head babies are found on a much heavier composition body than their European counterparts. Ball jointed bodies were also made but were usually of inferior quality.

Although the manufacture of bisque dolls' heads mainly finished when Germany once again flooded world markets in 1922, Japan continued to make small all bisque dolls, and some of these, made in occupied Japan, were even sold in Australia after the Second World War. These later small dolls were often of a quite inferior bisque, but were sold very cheaply in chain stores.

Jullien 1875–1904
An early dollmaker in France.

JULLIEN

1878 An award winner at the Paris Exposition.
1881 Purchased heads from François Gaultier.
1889 Factory was still in existence.
The bisque heads bearing the JULLIEN mark have paper-weight eyes, closed mouth and pierced ears.

Jumeau Paris and Montreuil-sous-Bois 1842–99
Pierre François Jumeau 1842–c. 1877
Emile Jumeau 1877–99 +
Pierre Jumeau made fashion type dolls with kid or wood bodies, with bisque heads that only had the size incised. Head sizes 0–9. In the late 1860s an incised J was used at the back of the head. Because it is situated at the base of the swivel neck and hard to read, it is often hard to determine whether it is an I or a J.

DÉPOSÉ
TÊTE JUMEAU
B⁰ᵗ SGDG

1867 Parisiennes and many other dolls were sold to overseas visitors who attended the 1867 Paris Exposition.
1873 Jumeau started making bisque dolls' heads; and soon after Emile Jumeau took over and began making Bébé Jumeau.

8
E J

The heads were made by pressing porcelain paste into two part plaster moulds that could only be used for fifty heads before definition was lost. Original firing lasted 27 hours and then, after painting, another 7 hours were needed in the kilns, but at a lower temperature. Jumeau made their own paperweight eyes.

1907

TÊTE JUMEAU

1878 The evolution of the Bébé. Early Bébés had bodies of wood with separate joints at shoulder, elbow, thigh and knee and in particular one piece lower arms. Because the legs were now stronger the Bébé could stand unaided. The so called 'Long Face Jumeau' heads were never marked except for size numbers on the head, Portrait Jumeaus were on eight balled jointed bodies which carried the Medaille d'Or stamp on the body.

1907
4

1879 Won medals for their dolls at Exhibition in Sydney.
1880 Won medals at Melbourne Exhibition for their dolls.
1881 Manufactured 85,000 dolls. The cost of the doll was based on the costuming, not the doll's head or body.

Jumeau Automata (red tick), *Newstead House, Brisbane*

Jumeau. *Private collection, NSW*

Open mouth Jumeau. *Private collection, NSW*

1907, all original. *Lesley Hurford collection*

Mark Depose/Tête Jumeau/Bte S.G.D.G. *Private collection, ACT*

1882 Heads were made with the ears moulded as part of the body on sizes 1–8, but from size 9–16 the ears were applied afterwards.

1883 Manufactured 115,000 Bébés.

1884 Made dolls with strings to pull to enable the doll to say Mama and Papa.

1885 All dolls now carried Jumeau trademarks.

1886 The Bébé Jumeau trademark was registered.

By the 1890s all their bisque heads were made by pouring the porcelain slip into the mould. The Tête Jumeau heads were made this way.

1890 Bébé Jumeau dolls were fully marked—on the back of the head, on the chemise, and if dressed on the left arm.

1892–1900 + Jumeau made bisque heads for use on the mechanical dolls made by Roullet & Decamps.

Over the years up to 30% of their trade was exports. Jumeau was never in conflict with Maison Bru, which was a smaller concern and posed no threat to Jumeau.

1893 Jumeau showed 25 bisque headed lady dolls dressed in historical costume at the Chicago Exposition. Manufactured a singing, talking doll that said up to 30 words. The whole doll was manufactured in the Jumeau factory.

1895 Jumeau and other French companies began to feel the impact of German dolls, particularly as labour costs were much higher in France. To reduce costs Jumeau had to lower the quality and these heads, of second and third quality, were not marked in the normal way or not marked at all. The high quality he had always insisted

1907, 64 cm (25″). *Courtesy J. Brooks, Quaint Collectables*

Princess Elizabeth, original clothes mark 21 UNIS FRANCE 149/306/Jumeau/1938 PARIS. *Lesley Hurford collection*

Jumeau sitting in her original box, original clothes, 21/S.F.B.J./301/Paris, Tête Jumeau (in red). *Courtesy Louisa K Dolls, Tahmoor NSW*

Princess Elizabeth, France, mark 306/JUMEAU. *Private collection, Queensland*

Original Jumeau chemise. *Private collection, Queensland*

on was gone, and the golden age of Jumeau was coming to an end.

1899 Dissolved the company on joining S.F.B.J. but the Jumeau name was still used as a trade name and trademark for years. On joining S.F.B.J. he received 1320 shares in the new company.

It must be noted that there are documented references for Jumeau's association with German manufacturers, such as Simon & Halbig for the supply of bisque heads for use by Jumeau.

It is interesting to muse over the fact that when the open mouthed Bébé Jumeau was produced, it was received enthusiastically, although it was sold at a dearer price than the closed mouth version. It is odd that today the closed mouth version is more collectable and brings almost double the price of the open mouth Jumeau.

1905–50s The Jumeau name could still be found on Bluette and Bambino dolls instead of S.F.B.J.

1938 Large Jumeau dolls were made for Princess Elizabeth and Princess Margaret of England. The dolls had bisque heads, composition bodies and a large wardrobe of clothes.

1940–50 Bisque heads, of different quality to earlier years, were still being produced and used on dolls, some with Jumeau marked heads, other with only paper tags or labels bearing Jumeau.

1958 The liquidation of S.F.B.J. and Jumeau occurred.

End of box lid of doll in box. *Courtesy Louisa K Dolls, Tahmoor NSW*

Princess Elizabeth, France, mark 306/JUMEAU.

Jumeau Fashion, Provincial costume, all original, 45 cm (18″), kid body, bisque lower arms. *Private collection, Brisbane*

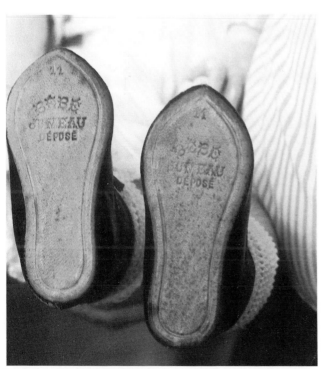

Bottom of Jumeau marked shoes on S.F.B.J./301/Paris, Tête Jumeau. *Courtesy Barry Brown, Louisa K Dolls, Tahmoor NSW*

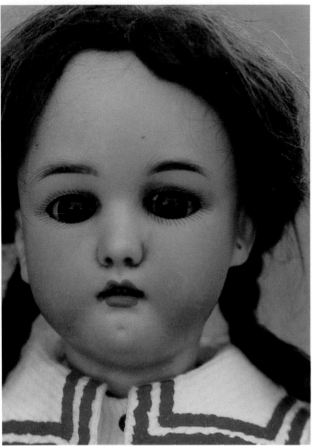

38 cm (15″), mark 1349/JUTTA/S&H/5. *Author's collection*

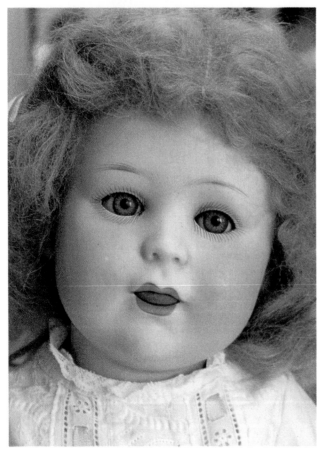

Mark JUTTA/1914/10. *Private collection, Brisbane*

Jutta

A line of dolls produced by Cuno & Otto Dressel using bisque heads manufactured by Simon & Halbig, Ernst Heubach and others.

The heads marked with Jutta were used on either baby or child dolls, with wigs or moulded hair, and some were fitted with flirty eyes.

K and K Toy Co. New York 1915–30 +

K and K Toy Co. was affiliated with the large American company Borgfeldt, and so German manufactured bisque dolls' heads can be found on dolls bearing the K and K tag.

Kaiser Baby

A name erroneously attached to the bisque headed baby doll by Kammer & Reinhardt with mould number 100, first produced in 1909. The domed dolls' head has painted eyes (not intaglio), open/closed mouth and a bent limb body which some thought resembled Kaiser Wilhelm as a baby. There is also a glass eyed version of this doll. So popular did this, the first character baby, become that many firms copied the doll.

Kammer & Reinhardt Walterhausen, Germany 1886–1933, doll factory

1885 Factory was founded by Ernst Kammer who was a sculptor and Franz Reinhardt, a merchant.

1886 Registered the company.

1889 Ernst Kammer made his first attempt at combining a doll and a gramophone, so that he would have an actual speaking doll.

1890 Advertised jointed dolls with bisque heads, porcelain bathing dolls with moveable arms and legs.

1893 Lauded at Chicago World Exhibition for their jointed dolls.

1894 Brought their gramophone doll onto the market.

1896 Registered K * R as a trademark for the fabrication, supply and export of dolls and all kinds of doll parts. Made bisque swimmers with moveable arms and legs.

1899 Was producing bisque doll heads that had genuine hair lashes.

1901 Ernst Kammer died. He had been responsible for many important innovations in the doll industry.

1902 Bought the firm of Heinrich Handwerck. This year was the beginning of the collaboration with Simon & Halbig. Registered Majestic Doll and Mein Liebling (117) as trademarks. Advertised that they had for sale walking dolls who could sit, stand, walk and move their heads from side to side. Brought the new idea of 'googly' eyes in dolls' heads from an invention by Gans & Seyfarth.

1903 Mein Liebling (My Darling) dolls (mould number 117); doll's head of finest bisque quality was patented. Also sold jointed dolls and walkers.

1905 Registered Mein Liebling as a trademark for dolls and
doll parts.

1909 The start of the character doll. Inspired by an
exhibition of art dolls at Munich, Franz Reinhardt had
a bronze bust sculpted by a Berlin artist of a six weeks
old baby. This was the first character head; afterwards
the artist sculpted other heads, which included Peter and
Marie (mould number 101). He found it possible to sell
only a few samples in Berlin in 1909, but received orders
worldwide for his innovation.

Following this success Karl Krauser sculpted the grand-
child of Franz Reinhardt, and this sculpture became
Hans and Gretchen (mould number 114).

1910 Hans and Gretchen were introduced at the Easter
Fair, Leipzig.

K ✡ R
SIMON & HALBIG
116/A

1912 Mein Liebling (mould number 117) was introduced.
The markings that were later to be associated with this
doll are as follows: 117 and 117A usually have closed
mouths, 117n and 117x open mouth with teeth. The 'n'
standing for neu (new) version was not made until after
1916.

1913 Max (mould number 123) and Moritz (mould number
124), two dolls with roguish eyes, were advertised as their
latest models.

Rare version K * R 100, only mark 1. Hair and glass eyes.
Private collection, Queensland

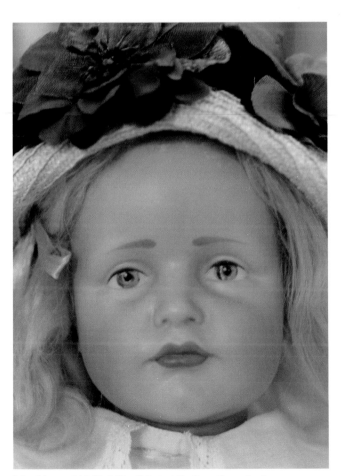

Mould no. 114 K * R. *Private collection, Queensland*

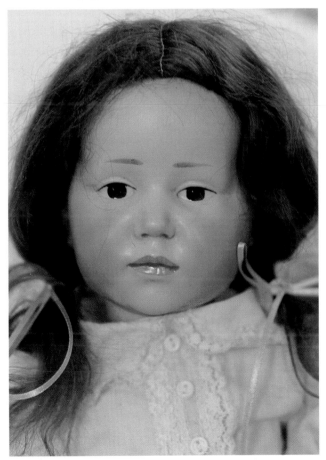

Mould no. 101 K * R. *Private collection, Queensland*

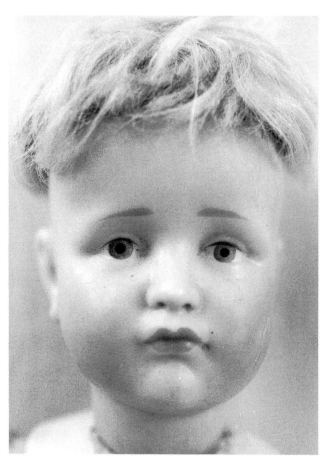

Original hair, mould no. 114 K * R.

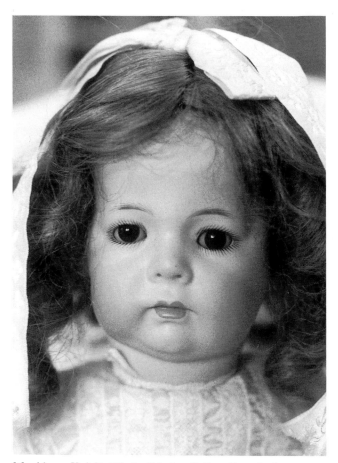

Mould no. K * R 115 A. *Private collection, Queensland*

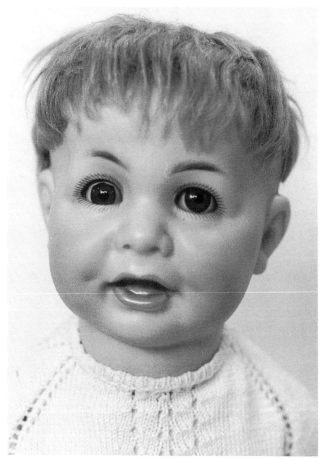

K * R 116A. *Private collection, Queensland*

K * R 116A. *Private collection, Queensland*

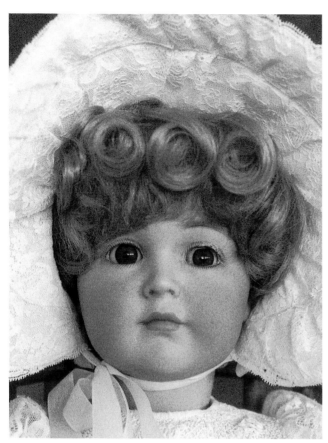

K * R 117. *Private collection, Taree*

Flirty eyes, K * R 117n. *Private collection, Queensland*

1916 Kammer & Reinhardt had become a joint-stock company and merged with the Bing organisation of Nuremberg. Invented a special doll's eye mechanism: when the doll's head was turned to the right the doll would sleep; when the head was turned to the left it would stay awake even when placed on its back.

HALBIG
K ✡ R
Germany

K ✡ R
SIMON&HALBIG
403
Germany

K ✡ R
SIMON & HALBIG
126

1918 The firm Schuetzmeister & Quendt supplied Kammer & Reinhardt with bisque dolls' heads.

1920 Kammer & Reinhardt bought the porcelain factory of Simon & Halbig.

1921 Registered Heinrich Handwerck Jointed Doll as a trademark.

1924 Used moveable rubber hands on some of their ball jointed dolls. Introduced the Mein Liebling baby (mould number 126).

1927 The Mein Liebling series, 117, 117a and 117n ball jointed dolls and baby doll 126, were all selling well.

1930 Kammer and Reinhardt were still part of the Bing concern, but owing to some trouble with Bing, their export business almost came to a standstill.

1933 Kammer & Reinhardt celebrated its 50th anniversary, although the company, the largest in the Walterhausen area in Northern Thuringia, had lost most of its influence and importance.

K * R 117n. *Private collection, Queensland*

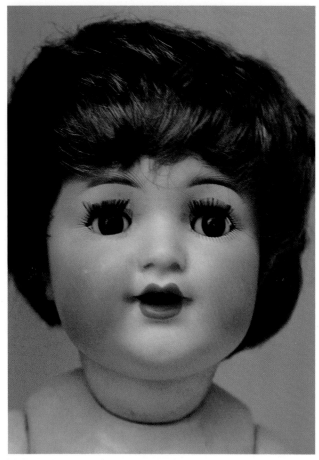

Mein Liebling Baby, K * R 126

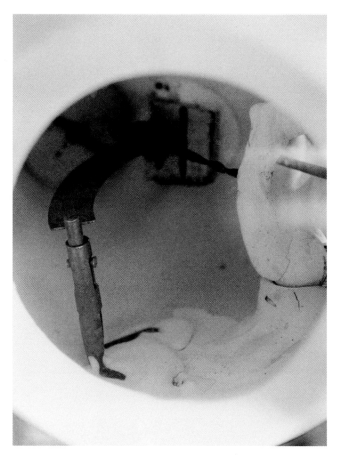

Eye mechanism that holds eye open when placed on one side, on K * R 126 head

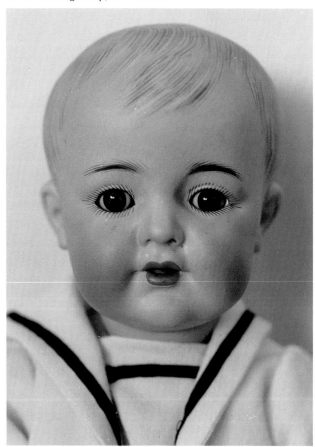

K * R 127/36. *Private collection, Queensland*

A simple guide to most of Kammer & Reinhardt's number series:

100 series Character dolls with socket heads.

200 series Shoulderplate bisque heads.

400 series Marked with S & H and K & R are bisque heads mainly found on walking dolls.

500 series Googly eyed bisque head dolls.

600 series Blacks and Mulattos.

Kammer and Reinhardt made all bisque child dolls, and small bisque head dolls with mohair wig, sleeping eyes, open or closed mouth, composition body with moulded and painted shoes and socks. One known mould number is 1126. The numbers often found at the base of the neck on Kammer & Reinhardt bisque heads are not mould numbers but refer to the size the doll should be approximately when attached to the body. Example: A bisque head with 66 on it, the doll should stand approximately 66 cm tall.

Kestner, J.D. Walterhausen, Germany 1823–1938, doll factory

H made in 12½ Germany J.D.K 211.

133 1 made in Germany

J.D.K. 237 made in Germany 31

Although the firm of J.D. Kestner dates from 1805, his dealings in dolls are only known from 1823.

J.D.K. 152/4. *In memory of Dorothy Bryce, Tamworth*

12-154.D1, Kestner, kid body

1840 At the Leipzig Fair he was the first toy maker from
Walterhausen. He went on to become the largest factory
owner in Walterhausen.

1841 Supplied Tauflings dressed only in a shift.

1858 J.D. Kestner died, but his widow and deputy directors
carried on the business.

1863 With Adolf Kestner as director, the firm was
producing dolls of papier mâché and wax.

1888 Kestner & Co. were making ball jointed dolls with
bisque heads, with or without wigs (moulded hair); cloth
or leather bodied dolls with bisque heads; bathing dolls
in bisque—with and without wigs; dolls' heads of bisque
and porcelain; child dolls with multicoloured dresses in
bisque (one-piece?). Early bisque heads with closed
mouths were unmarked except for X or XI and these
are credited to Kestner. Other early heads were those
of slightly turned head shoulderplate dolls.

1892 Dolls were marked with Made in Germany and a
mould number.

1893 Kestner showed special jointed dolls, bisque heads and
bathing dolls at the Chicago World Exhibition.

1896 The famous J.D.K. Germany (with crown) was
registered for dolls.
Leather bodied dolls, jointed dolls and dolls with cloth
bodies were produced and among the head moulds were
numbers 147, 148, 149, 154, 166, 195.

1898 Specialised in dolly face bisque dolls' heads with
jointed and kid bodies, bisque heads and all bisque dolls.

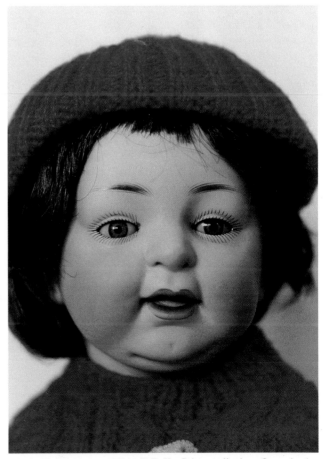

Mark H Germany 12/211/J.D.K. *Private collection, Queensland*

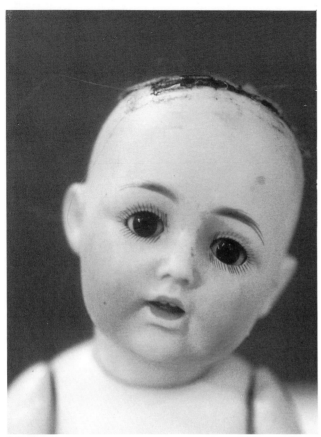

J.D.K.
247

Made some heads for Roullet & DeCamps walking dolls 1899–1914.

1897 Registered the Kestner Alphabet with marks such as B/6, C/7, D/8, etc. These are marks that can be found on Kestner bisque heads.

1910 c. Gibson Girl 172 was popular.

1914 Advertised Kewpies and the doll head Hilda, mould number 236, 237, which can also be in black 246, 247.

1918 Adolf Kestner died, but the factory was continued by long time employees.

1919 Firm had four new partners and was made a limited company.

1921 Proudly advertised finest jointed dolls, character babies, doll bodies, bisque doll heads, bisque bathing dolls, googly eyed dolls and Kewpies.

1923 Disposed of pre World War I stock to Latin America.

1932 A wide variety of bisque headed dolls and all bisque dolls were still being produced. Bent limb babies, Googlies, all bisque Kewpies, all bisque Max and Moritz, all bisque children with moulded boots, Frozen Charlotte types and dolls'-house dolls were among those produced.

1937 Still advertised babies and googly eyed dolls.

1938 The firm of Kestner was closed.

After World War I, the USA greatly influenced the design of dolls' heads, and Kestner supplied the following dolls: Bye-Lo Baby for George Borgfeldt. A series of baby heads for Century Doll Co. New York, mould numbers 279 and 281 (shoulderplate). Newborn Babies in all variations.

Original clothes, 26 cm (10″) mark Germany /J.D.K./257/24. *Author's collection*

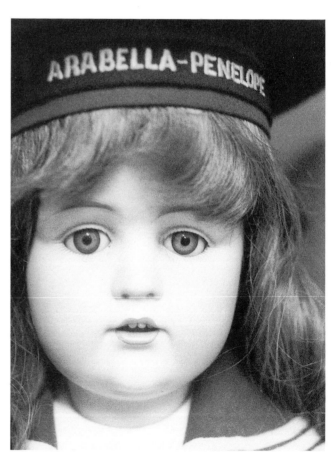

Mark 7½ Made in Germany 10½/J.D.K./249. *Private collection, Brisbane*

Kewpies from 1913 for George Borgfeldt. The Walkure (mould numbers 250, 292) was specially produced for Kley & Hahn, as were a series of character dolls for Catterfelder Puppenfabrik (mould numbers 200, 205, 207, 209, 270). Kestner also produced all bisque dolls in number series 100, 200 and 500. Often the heads and limbs were interchanged, and this is why many of these small dolls have an array of different numbers on them.

Numbers are 111, 122 (googly), 130, 141, 150, 179, 182 (Kestner Tiny Tot), 184, 185 (Kewpie), 186a (Max with moulded clothes—187a naked), 186b (Mortiz with moulded clothes—187b naked), 189 (googly), 192, 195, 196, 198. Those with the 200 number series were made as doll's-house dolls.

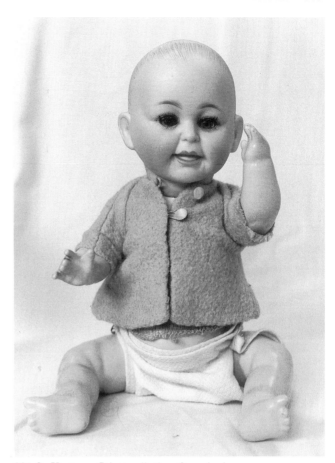

221 S. Kestner. *Private collection, Queensland*

Original clothes, mark S & C/J.D.K./257

J.D.K. 257, for S&C (Franz Schmidt)

240 Bisque headed, glass eyed, Kewpie character doll. Maker unknown, circa 1914. *Private collection, Queensland*

Kewpie 1912–32 +

These cute little figures representing cupids, drawn by Rose O'Neill for the *Ladies' Home Journal* and later the *American Woman's Home Companion*, proved very popular with the public.

By 1911 doll factories began writing to her asking for a real Kewpie doll, and whether she would model one in clay. She succeeded in doing just that. George Borgfeldt was fascinated by the Kewpie drawings and acquired from Rose O'Neill the rights to reproduce them in bisque.

The majority of Kewpies were made as one piece bodies, legs together, moveable arms, with eyes to the side and small moulded wings, normally blue, at the side of the neck or on the back of the body. Other Kewpie dolls were made with bisque socket heads on composition bodies or bisque flange necks on cloth bodies.

Kewpies were poured in bisque, in all sizes and poses. Most of them were depicted naked, with just a little red paper heart. Kestner was not able to meet the strong demand for these dolls, so by 1914 twenty-one other companies were engaged with their manufacture until the market was overwhelmed. Other makers of bisque Kewpies were Gbr. Voight, Herman Voight and Fulper Pottery. Japanese firms were found guilty of infringing copyright during World War I.

Kid bodies

Dolls' bodies were made of kid throughout the 19th century and into this century. The heads first fitted on to these bodies were the white china shoulderplate heads and later shoulderplate heads of bisque were used.

The earliest kid bodies had no joints, just the arms attached by sewing to the shoulder area, with sometimes the point of attachment covered by the shoulderplate. During the 1860s and the era of the Fashion or Lady doll, the kid bodies were made with gussets to give the doll more flexibility. Probably the most perfect kid body to emerge during this era was the blown kid body sold by Madame Clement.

The firm of Bru used kid bodies on their Circle Dot and Bru Jne dolls.

Kid bodies were popular with many German and some French firms from the 1880s until the 1920s, especially after the introduction of the rivet joint or Ne Plus Ultra hip joint for kid bodies. The joint used metal buttons and wires in the hip or knee area, usually with bisque forearms and cloth lower legs.

During World War I both Japan and England used a substitute kid called Kidlyn (oiled cloth) with their bisque shoulderplate heads. Some cheaper quality German dolls can also be found of this material.

Although the very early kid bodied dolls have beautifully formed hands in kid, the later dolls relied on coloured or white bisque forearms, some even had celluloid forearms. See 'Bodies' for photographs of various kid bodies.

Kley & Hahn Ohrdruf, Germany 1902 +, doll factory

1902 The factory was founded by Albert Kley and Paul Hahn with fifteen workers.

1903 Advertised an opening special of ball jointed dolls with bisque heads of their own design. Registered the Walküre trademark. The heads were made by Kestner.

1910 Character dolls, either boy or girl, were advertised with closed mouths and painted eyes. Claimed they had been making character dolls since 1907.

1911 Double faced character baby. Participated at the Leipzig Fair with ball jointed dolls and shoulderplate heads on leather bodies.

> K&H
> Germany
> 169

Special
Made in Germany

Walküre
Germany

1915 Bisque heads modelled to represent Frenchmen, Englishmen and Blacks of Senegal as well as character heads were produced.

1922 Albert Kley died.

1926 Jointed dolls and character babies were still being advertised at various prices.

The Kley and Hahn mould number 135 domed bisque head is often mistaken for the K * R 100 mould. Marks used differentiated between products for German speaking customers (Spezial) and English speaking (Special).

Other moulds used were: Double faced baby—mould 159

Kley & Hahn, two faced baby

Two faced baby. *Leslie Hurford collection*

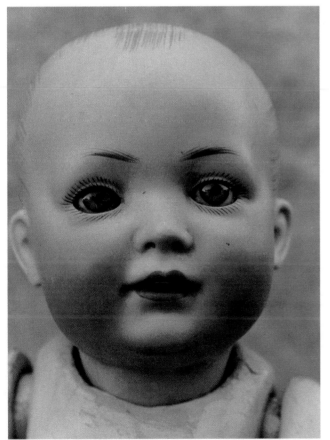

Kley & Hahn, bisque head made by Bahr & Proschild, mark
532. *Author's collection*

Teenage body, mark Kley & Hahn/Walkure/46. *Lesley
Hurfood collection*

Gbr. Knoch, mark 185 18/0. *Private collection, Ipswich, Queensland*

Lanternier, mark A.L. & Cie/Cherie/8. *Private collection, Brisbane*

or unmarked, thought to have been manufactured by Hertel Schwab. The 200 mould and Walkure by Kestner with 250, 282, 292 being the most common.

100 series, character heads by Hertel Schwab & Co, were mainly dome headed dolls with numbers 138, 158, 160, 167, 176, 525, 531.

500 series were made by Bahr & Proschild.

Kling, C.F. & Co. Ohrdruf, Germany 1870 + , porcelain factory

1870 Although Kling & Co. was founded in 1834, it wasn't until 1870 that dolls became part of their production. Made bisque and china shoulderplate heads from the same moulds. Made bisque heads with moulded hair, flowers, jewellery and parts of blouses as part of head.

1886 First class dolls' heads and dolls and bathing dolls were advertised.

1893 Produced bisque doll heads, dolls and bathing dolls.

1911 Showed bisque children, dolls' heads and bathing dolls at Leipzig Fair. Their all bisque children were jointed at shoulders and hips, wigged with glass eyes and closed mouths, and strap moulded boots with heels.

1921 Participated in the Leipzig Fair showing porcelain dolls, dolls'-house dolls and porcelain heads.
The Kling factory was one of the firms that produced Bye-Lo baby heads.

1930 Porcelain dolls and heads were advertised.

1941 Still referred to as manufacturing porcelain dolls.

Mark Normally a K within a bell.

Knoch, Gebruder Neustadt, Germany 1887–1919, porcelain factory

1887 Founded by the Knoch brothers, Ernst the dollmaker and Christian the merchant. Produced bisque doll heads.

1913 Produced bisque doll heads, socket and shoulderplate, with or without hairstyles, with stationary or sleeping eyes. Also made character dolls.

1919 The factory was taken over by Max Oscar Arnold. The bisque heads, shoulderplate or socket, were normally marked with crossed bones and G.K.N. (Gebruder Knoch Neustadt). Many character heads have no marking at all except Ges. Nr. Gesch with a number.

Koenig & Wernicke Walterhausen, Germany 1912 + , doll factory.

1912 Max Koenig and Rudolf Wernicke, who had both worked with other doll factories, became the new owners. They manufactured jointed dolls, babies and toddler dolls.

1914 Max Koenig left the firm.

1919 Rudolf and Paul Wernicke were the owners.

1920 Manufactured bisque headed dolls and babies.

1924 Paul Wernicke founded his own firm.

Bisque heads were supplied by Bahr & Proschild, Hertel Schwab & Co., and Armand Marseille. Known mould numbers are 98, 99, 100, 1070.

Kuhnlenz, Gebruder A.G. Kronach, Germany, porcelain factory

1884 Founded by Julius, Cuno and Bro Kuhnlenz to produce doll heads.

1891 Manufactured bisque dolls' heads.

1895 Doll heads were marked with 'dep'.

1901 Julius Kuhnlenz left the company.

1910 Bisque doll heads and bathing dolls were produced by firm.

1935 Factory was shut down.

The mark Gbr. with 165, or Gbr K in a sun with numbers such as 41, 44 and size number, was once thought to be that of Gbr. Krauss.

Lady or Fashion dolls

Nearly all the bisque heads found on Fashion or Lady dolls were made by pressing the porcelain paste into the head moulds. Some of the Lady dolls were made with painted eyes and stationary necks on their shoulderplates, but most had glass eyes—many of them paperweight—and a swivel neck with a separate shoulderplate.

The dolls' heads were marked or unmarked, some with only numerals. The only means of identification with many of these dolls was the name of the store where they were sold, printed directly on their kid bodies, or paper stickers attached to their bodies.

The type of clothes, particularly the beautiful clothes resembling the latest French mode, earned for this type of doll the name Lady or Fashion doll. Some were even referred to as Parisiennes, for example by Emile Jumeau. This name was also reinforced by the womanliness often found in their many body shapes.

Both French and German porcelain factories made heads for Lady dolls, among them being Bru, Jumeau and Simon & Halbig.

Lanternier, A. & Cie Limoges, France 1915–24, porcelain factory

FABRICATION
FRANÇAISE

AL E Cⁱᵉ
LIMOGES
Cherie.

The Lanternier factory was engaged in manufacturing bisque dolls' heads and dolls. Some of the names used in conjunction with their mark are Caprice, Chérie, Favorite, La Georgienne, Lorraine and Toto. A stylised anchor was also part of their trademark.

Many of the dolls were dressed in French Provincial costumes of Alsace, Arles and Bourg. In 1924 Lanternier was renowned for the lovely heads on its dolls.

Sèvres selected Lanternier, one of three factories, to help them in the production of dolls' heads in the years 1915 and 1916.

Lanternier, mark A.L. & Cie. *Private collection, Brisbane*

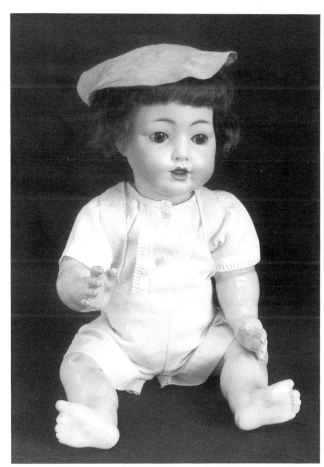

Koenig & Wernicke. *Photograph courtesy Jacki Brooks, Goulburn*

Leather bodies see Kid bodies

Limbach, A.G. Limbach, Germany 1893–1937, porcelain factory

1893 Showed dolls and bathing dolls at the World Exhibition in Chicago. Beautiful dolls' heads were produced at Limbach around 1893, when they produced bisque doll heads, jointed dolls, dolls'-house dolls and bathing dolls.

1910 Manufactured small jointed dolls, with or without dresses, bathing dolls, character dolls and all bisque dolls.

1919 The making of dolls' heads was started again. Registered Limbach Puppen (Limbach dolls) as a trademark. From 1919 heads were marked with the Limbach cloverleaf.

1926 Specialised in jointed dolls and doll heads.

1937 Factory was still producing babies, bathing dolls and dolls.

Lori see Swaine & Co.

Marseille, Armand Koppelsdorf, Germany 1890–1930 + , porcelain factory

Armand Marseille was the most prolific of all the German dollmakers and the quality of the enormous range of heads that he produced at Koppelsdorf was consistently excellent. It is because of the vast amount of dolls that were manufactured and sent to Australia, that these dolls of such high quality can still be bought at a reasonable price except for his rarer mould numbers. Probably the most common mould numbers found in Australia in connection with Armand Marseille would have to be his mould number 390 with all its many variations and sizes, followed by mould number 351—flange neck baby head with open mouth. This baby head can be found on a variety of bodies, due to the fact that they were imported mainly as heads and made up in small workrooms or factories here in Australia.

Born in St Petersburg Russia in 1856, Armand Marseille bought a toy factory in Koppelsdorf. He took over the trademark of Mathias Lambert—an anchor—and later registered it in many different variations.

   1894 AM DEP

1890 First experimented in manufacturing bisque heads for dolls. Known to have made the mould number 390 (which only means socket head) about this date, and this mould number continued until 1938.

1892 Manufactured shoulderplate heads for Cuno & Otto Dressel.

1893 Produced fine bisque dolls and jointed bathing dolls.

1901 Manufactured Floradora marked dolls for George Borgfeldt.

Limbach, crown and shamrock-1772

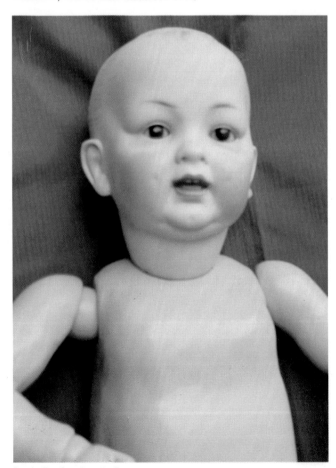

Lori. By Swaine & Co.

Bodies found on flange neck A.M. Dream Babies, from left: Laurie Cohen body; straight legged cloth body, composition hands; frog leg cloth body, celluloid hands

Dream Baby A.M. 341 and the original layette made for the doll

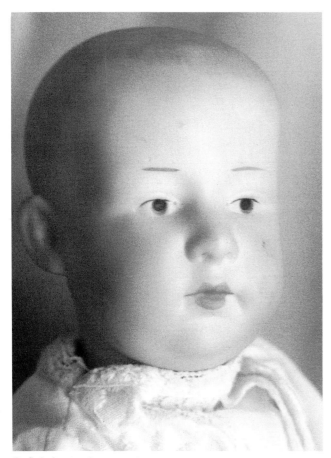

Definitely not the normal A.M. 341. *Private collection, Armidale*

Markings on back of head of unusual A.M. 341

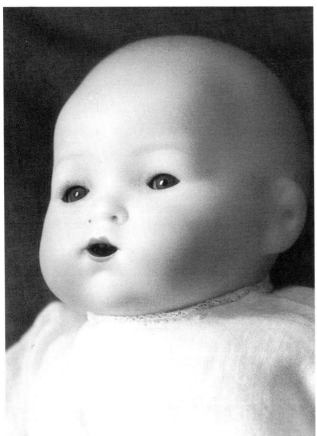

Unusual A.M. 341—should be a closed mouth, has had mouth cut out and painted when manufactured. *Vera Woodhead collection*

1910 Various anchor trademarks for doll heads were registered.

The following mould numbers were introduced: 500—domed head, painted eyes, closed mouth; 520—domed head, sleeping eyes, open mouth; 560A—socket head, sleeping eyes, open mouth; 600—domed shoulderplate, painted eyes, closed mouth; 620, 621, 630, 640a—all shoulderplate heads with painted eyes, closed mouth; 800—socket head, sleeping eyes, open mouth.

Made in Germany
Armand Marseille
390n
DRGM 246/1
A 2/0xM

Made in Germany
Floradora
A 5 M

3200
AM   DEP

1912 390n, Fany and mould numbers 250 and 252.

1913 Mould number 401, a lady doll for Louis Wolf & Co.

1919 Armand Marseille retired, and son Herman took over. Herman Marseille and Ernst Heubach Jnr combined their two factories into United Kopplesdorf Porcelain Manufactuary. However the two companies continued to manufacture dolls' heads separately under their own trademarks.

1924 Introduced A.M. Dream Baby 351 (open mouth) and 341 (closed mouth) versions.

1925 Armand Marseille died.

1926 Manufactured the Baby Phyllis line of dolls.

1930 Specialised in manufacturing porcelain dolls' heads. Supplied mould numbers 390, 520 and 1330 to Wilhelm Muller.

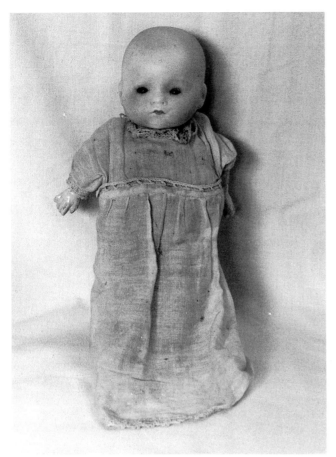

Dream Baby, original as sold, mark A.M. 341. *Private collection, Queensland*

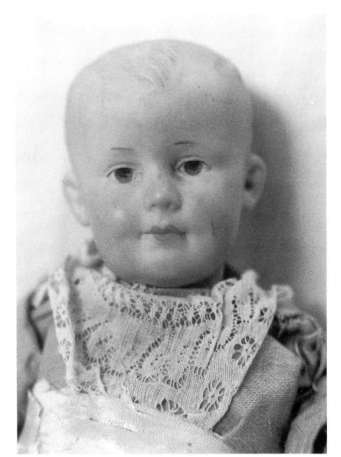

A.M. -500, Germany, A. 2/0 M. *Private collection, Queensland*

1932 The joint company was disbanded and once again became the separate firms of Marseille and Heubach.

1937 Still producing bisque doll heads.

1950 + Producing dolls in G.D.R. (East Germany) in a ceramic type composition.

Armand Marseille produced doll heads with their own trademarks and mould numbers as well as filling innumerable orders for USA companies, some Australian wholesalers and retailers and many factories in Germany, including:

George Borgfeldt, USA Mould nos 250, 251, 252, 253, 259, 327, 328, 329, Just Me 310.

Cuno & Otto Dressel, Germany Mould nos 93, 341 (Dream Baby), 1776, 1892, 1894, 1896, 1898.

Maar & Sohn Mould no. 256.

Emil Pfeiffer Mould no. 560a.

Louis Amberg Mould nos 371, 972, Baby Peggy 973.

Peter Scherf Mould nos 1899, 1901, 1902.

Gbr. Eckardt Mould nos 540, 992 Our Pet.

Otto Gans Mould nos 970, 975.

Seyfarth & Reinhardt Mould no. 995 with SUR.

Hugo Wiegand Mould no. 1231.

Louis Wolf & Co. Mould nos 401, 121, 975.

Baby Phyllis Doll Co. Mould no. 240.

Arranbee, USA Rock-a-bye Mould nos 341, 351.

L.C. Cohen, Australia Mould nos 341, 351, 352, 382, 384.

Hitz Jacobs & Kassler Kiddie Joy Mould nos 345, 372, 375, 991, 993, 997.

Wilhelm Muller Mould nos 520, 1330.

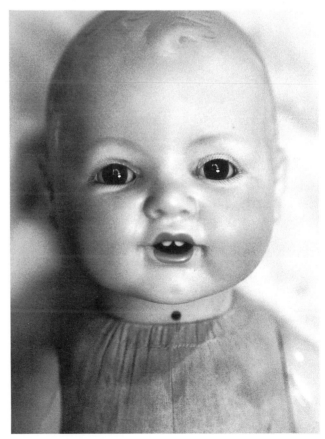

Australian Laurie Cohen cloth body, celluloid limbs, mark A.M. 384. *Dorothy Boland collection*

Ellar by Armand Marseille

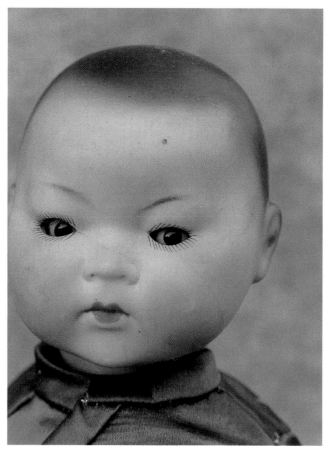

Composition body, mark A.M. 353 (oriental). *Author's collection*

Rare pate cut and wigged A.M. 341. *Lesley Hurford collection*

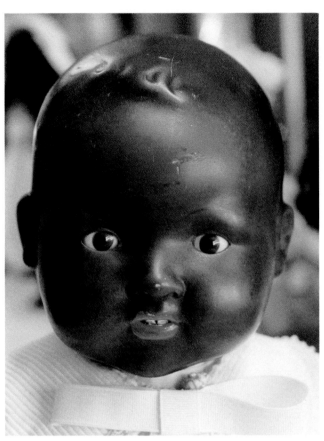

Black A.M. 351. *Betty Brown collection*

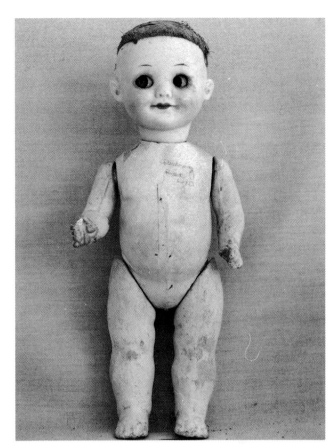

Googly, composition toddler body, mark A.M. 323. *Private collection, Queensland*

There were many other numbers manufactured by this firm, still to be found and photographed, such as the mould number 384 that has surfaced in the last few years here in Australia—a baby doll with its body made here and the doll assembled in a small doll factory in Sydney in the 1930s. Anomalies are also surfacing as more and more collectors are becoming aware of their dolls and their histories. Such an example is the 341 mould number Dream Baby found with an open mouth instead of a closed mouth, and the domed head, painted eye doll with the 341 number.

Many collectors are unaware of the meaning of letters on their baby dolls' heads—K (kurbelkopf) means socket head-domed head, Ka socket head cut out to take a wig and X reduced intermediate size. Number only on 341, 351 etc refers to a flange neck.

M (in a stylised five leaf clover) Japan 1915–22
One of the marks found on Japanese bisque heads produced during the First World War. Unfortunately as of yet their manufacturer is not known.

Marotte
This is a small doll's head atop a stick; as the stick was twirled a concealed music maker or bells made a noise. Sometimes a whistle was incorporated in the base of the stick, which could be of ebony or ivory. Many of these 'folies' had bisque heads. Despite the cheapness of many of these doll-like toys, they were dressed in colourful silks with ribbons and gold and silver fringing. A fancy jester

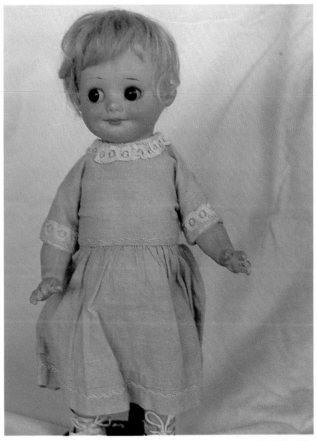

Old dress, original hair and shoes, mark Germany/323/A 4/0 M. *Private collection, Brisbane*

Just Me, mark A.M. 310. *Courtesy J. Brooks, Quaint Collectables*

Shoulderplate, kid body, mark A.M. 370. *Author's collection*

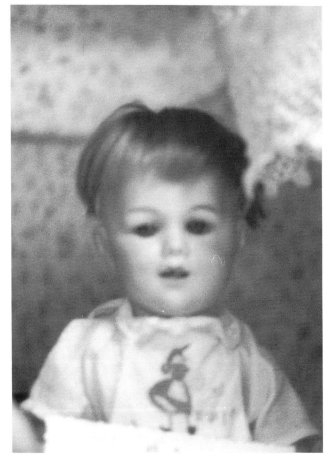

Mark A.M./980. *Lesley Hurford collection*

Mignon, Germany. *Photograph courtesy D. Gilliland*

Rosebud by Armand Marseille. Shoulderplate, cloth body, mark Rosebud/A. 8/OM/Made in Germany. *Private collection, Queensland*

Armand Marseille flange neck on Laurie Cohen body, original clothes, mark A.M. 382. *Private collection, Gulgong*

type hat was worn on the head. Gottlieb Zinner & Sohne of Schalkau and Rabery & Delphieu of France both produced Marottes.

Mein Liebling (My Darling)
A name used by Kammer & Reinhardt in conjunction with their dolls with the 117 and 126 mould numbers.
117 and 117a are a bisque headed doll with jointed body, the head having sleeping eyes and an open mouth.
117n is on a ball jointed body, with sleeping eyes, but has an open mouth.
Both these types of dolls can have flirty eyes.
126—known as Mein Leibling Baby—has a bisque head on a baby body, with sleeping eyes (often flirty) and an open mouth.

Mignon

The word Mignon was used in two trademarks registered by Felix Arena from 1918–20. An incised line drawing of an early biplane was also included in the trademark. The 53 cm (21″) doll had a bisque head with sleeping eyes, open mouth and a mohair wig and was sold on a fully jointed composition body.

Marotte, A.M. head. *Lesley Hurford collection*

Marotte. *Private collection*
Different carved handles, bells for noise

M.O.A. see Arnold, Max Oscar

Modern bisque china dolls

In the late 1970s Korea and Taiwan began producing simple matt 'china' or rather poor quality bisque shoulderplate headed dolls dressed in simple cotton frocks and bonnets. The shoes or boots were often moulded as part of the lower legs. These dolls have greatly improved over the last twelve or so years and many are sold as limited editions. Brands such as Hillview Lane and Primrose Hill and also the Heritage Dolls at the moment available through Coles are putting new names into the doll world. Other companies are also offering limited editions of fairy-tale dolls. All these dolls still have to find their place in the resale market.

Modern doll artist dolls

The bisque headed dolls that have been sculpted by recognised doll artists here in Australia and in Germany and the United States are often beautiful characterisations of children and are gaining in popularity with many collectors because of their more lifelike look and cuteness of face. Dolls by these recognised artists can be expensive as they are normally sold in very limited editions.

Many of these dolls are also being offered as moulds for reproduction by students at doll making studios in a slightly smaller version, so that many of these popular dolls, such as Barefoot Bébés and children and also Punkin and Bubbles and many others, can be found in abundance at most doll fairs. These dolls should have the copyright mark of the

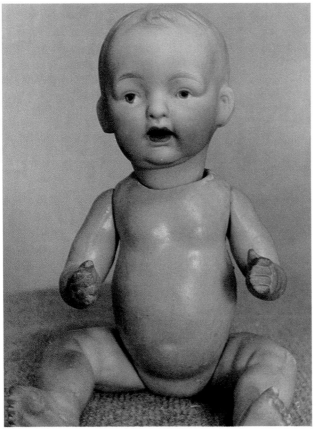

30 cm (12″), mark M (in Shamrock) Nippon. *Ipswich, Queensland*

Morimura Bros, painted eyes, mark 2/MB/Japan/2/0.
Courtesy Discovery Corner, Brisbane

original doll artist as well as the initials of the reproduction maker on the back of the head, plus the date they were reproduced.

Morimura Bros Japan and USA 1915–22

At the outbreak of World War I there was considerable consternation amongst the dealers and wholesalers who supplied dolls to the American and Australian market as to where they could purchase the so beloved bisque head dolls of the time.

Morimura Bros, a leading Japanese import business, promptly moved to fill the gap. Experts were engaged and sent to Japan to build a factory for manufacturing bisque headed dolls.

By 1916 most of the problems had been overcome and Morimura Bros were able to produce bisque dolls' heads that attracted considerable attention. They were so successful that their output was sold a year before the delivery date. In 1918 they were offering bisque headed dolls with sleeping eyes, Kidlyn bodies and jointed hips and arms. Bisque babies of all descriptions were also being sold.

They continued advertising their bisque dolls in 1921, then in 1922 the German dolls returned to world markets.

Moulded hair

This term means that the hair on the head has been moulded as an integral part of the head mould. The early shoulder-plate heads of china, 'parian' or bisque nearly all had moulded hair in various styles. As most of these early shoulderheads were not marked in any way, it is the style of their moulded hairdos that helps identify the age of these dolls to a certain degree.

Black painted hair is the most common colour found on the glazed china heads, but blonde is more popular on the matt finished shoulderplate heads known as parian or bisque.

A large majority of the all bisque dolls and bisque Frozen Charlottes were made with moulded hair.

The domed heads of many character dolls, on closer examination, are usually found to be moulded, some to a greater extent than others. Some prime examples are the character dolls by Kammer & Reinhardt, S.F.B.J. and Gebr. Heubach.

Nancy Ann see Storybook Dolls

Oberender, Nikolaus Oeslau 1910–27, porcelain manufacturer

NB
Germany
121

1910 A porcelain factory was founded by Nikolaus Oberender and reference was made to him manufacturing bisque dolls.
1927 Had a new partner Wilhelmine Oberender.

Ohlhaver, Gebruder Sonneberg 1912–30 +, doll factory
1912 The firm was founded.
1913 Advertised ball jointed dolls with Revalo on the head.

Morimura Bros, sleeping glass eyes, mark MB/Japan. *Lesley Hurford collection*

Pair of bisque dolls with moulded hairstyles. *Courtesy David Parry, Melbourne*

The name Revalo was devised by taking the name of the owner, Ohlhaver, removing both 'h's and then turning the name back to front—Reva (h) l (h) o. Revalo was used on toddlers, bent limb babies and dolls with socket and shoulderplate heads.

1921 Revalo, My Queen Doll and Bébé Princess were names used in advertising.

1925 Reported that 500 dozen Revalo dolls were produced per week.

The Coquette mould would be the most famous mould by this firm. Revalo heads were produced by Ernst Heubach, Gbr. Heubach and the porcelain factory at Mengersgereuth.

Ondine the Swimming Doll 1876-1929
Benoit was a doll and toy maker in Paris, and is now known for his most famous mechanical doll, the swimming doll which was sold under the name Ondine.

He obtained a French patent for the mechanism in 1876 and in 1878 English, German and United States patents were also obtained.

He exhibited at the Paris Exposition in 1878 and in Melbourne in 1880 where he received a certificate for his display.

An advertisement in 1890 credited him with fourteen French or foreign patents and Gold and Silver medal awards for

Head made by Gbr. Heubach, mark
10727/Revalo/Germany/7½. *Private collection, Townsville*

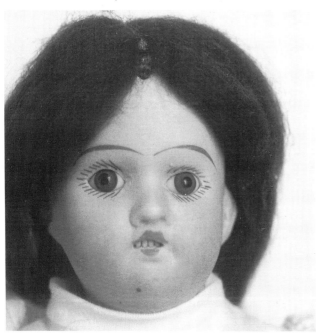

Nikolaus Oberender, 23 cm (9"), mark NO/121/13/0. *Doreen Budd collection*

Painted or sprayed bisque, mark Armand Marseille/Germany/390 *Armidale, NSW*

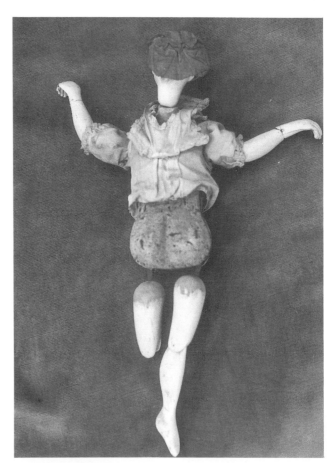

Ondine, the mechanical swimmer designed by Elim Martin, Paris. Bisque head by Simon & Halbig 1079, cork body, carved wooden legs and arms, metal hands. Portion original clothing. *Private collection*

Painted/sprayed bisque, original clothes, mark Armand Marseille/1330/. *Private collection, Queensland*

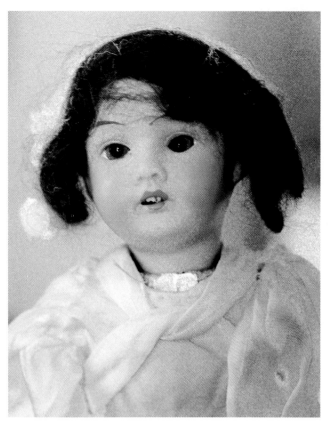

Sprayed or painted bisque, all original, dressed as bride, simple carton body, 1920s, 25 cm (10″). Recknagel, mark Germany R/A 11/0R. *Author's collection*

Painted/sprayed bisque, mark 16/0. *Courtesy Doll & Toy Collection, Brisbane*

his mechanical toys. Also in the 1890 advertisement Eli Martin was credited as being the inventor of Ondine. Many of the Ondine dolls were fitted with Simon & Halbig bisque heads and the 1079 mould number. The mechanism is surrounded by cork, the arms are wood with metal hands, and the legs are carved wood. Some of these dolls were still being produced in 1929.

Oriental and exotic dolls

With the continual expansion during the 19th century of the colonial empires of France, Germany and particularly Great Britain there was a demand for dolls that represented these far-flung colonial outposts. Because of this demand nearly all doll factories manufactured oriental or exotic bisque headed dolls with colouring quite distinct from the lovely complexions of their normal doll range. Special techniques had to be developed to achieve even tinting of the bisque heads and bodies from the darkest black to the brightest brown to represent black and mulatto dolls. Various shades of yellow were used to represent the various Asian regions in many bisque doll heads.

By 1893 Theodor Recknagel had applied for a patent that included colouring the porcelain used in manufacturing doll heads.

At first many factories offered doll models in white or tinted, with the coloured heads just being differently painted. Dark glass eyes, dark wigs to suit the negroid type of doll and straight dark hair for the Asiatic doll completed the illusion. Dolls with Burmese, Arabian, Indian, Japanese and Chinese characteristics were achieved by the appropriate tinting of the bisque porcelain and by making the moulds of the faces more comfortable to the races represented. By 1893 Simon & Halbig had registered moulds numbers 1098 and 1107 representing a Chinese child's countenance. Bahr & Proschild also produced similar heads. Really stylish oriental character dolls were produced and sold between 1910 and 1920, with the heads painted to look quite realistic. The most convincing models of this type of doll were produced by Armand Marseille and J.D. Kestner.

Painted or sprayed bisque

A term commonly used in connection with bisque headed dolls that were mainly manufactured in the 1930s. Some black and oriental dolls' heads were also painted. Because of economic conditions in the 1930s, and the cost and time involved in producing permanent fired in colouring in bisque heads, a cheaper method was required. Bisque heads were spraypainted, giving a much brighter hue, and with eye shadow obviating the need for painted eyelashes this was a much faster process. Some of these painted or sprayed heads were given a minimum of heat to set the paint, others were not; so unfortunately many of these heads lose their colour very easily and care should be taken with these dolls. The dolls' heads are usually the same as those with fired in colour so are still quite collectable, with sleeping glass eyes, wigs and jointed bodies. Great care should be taken when removing a wig for any reason as the old glue is inclined to lift the sprayed paint; and *never* subject these dolls to *water*.

Parian

Many collectors erroneously called unglazed china dolls 'parian'. This name has been used in particular in regard to the matt finished, rather white, moulded hairdo shoulder-plate heads of last century. Such heads should be called bisque, as parian is a name used to describe a type of half-vitreous porcelain, resembling Carrara marble, which originated in England in 1848. It was mainly used for statues and figures, and because of its composition was found too hard and brittle for use in dolls' heads.

Parian type

Dolls that are referred to as parian are actually made of a very fine white bisque consisting of 40 parts felspar, 36 parts china clay and 24 parts frit (very fine ground glass). This mixture gives the head a beautiful finish. Parian dolls' heads are without the pink tinting or underblush found on the later dolly-faced dolls produced in bisque. Nearly all true parian dolls have beautifully sharp, rather likelike features and finely defined hairstyles, with the only colouring being that found on the hair, cheeks, lips and eyes, although some of these dolls are found with glass eyes. All are shoulderplate heads.

It was found that glazing these early dolls, as was common with china heads, disguised the fine detail incorporated in the fancy hairstyles and neck ornamentation, so the heads were fired and then delicately painted, to retain the marble-like look they were aiming at.

A great number of the commercially produced bodies for these early parian heads were made of leather or cloth with leather hands. Later dolls had parian type limbs and some

dolls' bodies were made at home as many of the later dolls' heads were readily available.

Quite a few of these dolls were made with parts of the heads such as the hair and the ornamentation, either on the hair or on the shoulderplate, receiving an extra glaze fire, thus you can find both parian and bisque dolls that have moulded hair with this type of treatment.

By general consensus the beautiful and exquisite early dolls with the fine white matt finish are known as parian, whereas the later and rather more porous heads with poorer finish are probably better described as 'blonde bisque' or 'untinted bisque', depending on which is in fashion at the time.

Pate

A very important part of most of the old bisque headed dolls, this is the name given to the piece of material placed over the hole that was cut in the top of the dolls' head when it was first being produced. Onto the pate is usually glued the wig, or in the case of the very old bisque headed dolls made in France, the wigs were tacked onto the cork pate with very small tacks.

The pate can be made of cork (used by many of the early French dollmakers), wood, plaster (a specialty of the Kestner firm in Germany), or simply a concavely pressed piece of cardboard in a size suitable to cover the hole in the back of the head and also reach out to the edge of the head in most cases. A replacement pate should only be tacked to the head in a maximum of four places so that it can easily be lifted for examination of the inside of the head or the eyes.

Pfeiffer, Emil Vienna, Austria 1873–1925 + , dressed dolls

1873 The factory was founded.
1926 The company was reorganised and called Emil Pfeiffer & Sons, and at that time also had a branch Gbr. Pfeiffer in Sonneberg, Germany.

Marks found on dolls have E and P intertwined, and the word Husby.

Pfeiffer, Gebruder Kopplesdorf, Germany, doll and toy factory
1923 Advertised Husby dressed doll.
1925 Advertised their Hanka mark for Ma-ma dolls and new-born babies, also walking and talking dolls.

Branch of Emil Pfeiffer, Vienna.

Phénix Bébé

PHENIX
☆95 ⟨BÉBÉ PHENIX⟩ PHÉNIX-BABY

A trademark registered in 1899 by Mettais, who was head of the Jules Steiner firm from 1899 to approximately 1905. E. Daspres was listed as head of Jules Steiner from 1906. Mettais used the trademark Phénix Bébé on his dolls, and Phenix Baby for the English speaking market.

Group of Piano babies, Gbr. Heubach. *Lesley Hurfood collection*

Piano Baby, Gbr. Heubach. *Lesley Hurford collection*

Phonograph dolls

Following the success of Thomas Edison's invention, a dream could become a reality. A doll could be made that would imitate the human voice.

The Edison Phonograph doll first went into mass production in 1889 with a Simon & Halbig bisque head.

In 1884 Jumeau made his own version of the phonograph, but because of the high cost few were sold. At the 1894 Leipzig Toy Fair Kammer and Reinhardt introduced their phonograph doll using a procedure invented by Emil Berliner, but unfortunately it was discontinued due to malfunction.

Piano Babies

These are beautifully sculpted and made, small one-piece bisque figures with moulded hair or wigs. They are normally portrayed wearing painted white chemises with blue borders. The firm of Gebruder Heubach specialised in manufacturing a vast variety, both in size and shape, of these winsome characters.

Pincushion dolls see Half dolls

Pintel & Godchaux Montreuil, France 1890–99

P G

$$\overset{C}{P\,1\overset{\cdot}{3}\,G}$$
DÉPOSE

1890 Formed a partnership. They vied with Fleischmann & Bloedel in making 'cheap articles'.

Manufactured dolls, but the bisque heads used on their dolls were made by another French firm, Gaultier Frères. Displayed their dolls at the Chicago Exposition. Became one of the founder members of S.F.B.J. in 1899. *Mark* P.G.

P.M. see Porzellanfabrik Mengersgereuth

Porcelain or bisque

Some confusion arises out of the use of the word porcelain in conjunction with dolls. It probably derives from the fact that it is porcelain paste or slip that was used to manufacture dolls' heads. In the years prior to 1880 most dolls' heads were manufactured using porcelain paste, a kneaded smooth paste that was pressed into the doll moulds. Later technology enabled porcelain slip to be poured into the moulds, the same method that is used by dollmakers today.

The main variations of the name should refer to the actual doll's head finish:

China A doll head that has been painted, fired and then glazed to give a high shiny finish. This type of head was particularly popular in the early and middle portion of last century, and nearly all the doll heads in this manner are shoulderplate heads.

Bisque A doll head with a matt finish. It would have been pressed or poured, fired, painted the delicate colour required and then fired again, finishing with a smooth matt finish. This is the finish on nearly all Bébés, and German and French dolls with socket heads from the 1870s to the end of the 1930s.

Parian see Parian

Unfortunately, in many reference books, particularly German, when porcelain is mentioned you have to check the mould numbers to see whether it was a glazed (china) or matt (bisque) finish.

Rabery & Delphieu, France

Rabery & Delphieu, all original. *Private collection, Brisbane*

Porzellanfabrik Mengersgereuth. Baby body, 48 cm (19″), mark P.M./914 Germany/9.

Porzellanfabric Burggrub see Schoenau, Arthur and Schoenau & Hoffmeister

Porzellanfabrik Mengersgereuth Mengersgereuth, Germany 1908-30+, porcelain factory

1908 Firm founded by Carl Craemer and François E. Heron, and registered a trademark for porcelain goods.
1913 New owners—Robert Carl and Gustav Liebermann; reference was made to dolls' heads.
1920 Employed 125 workers, reference to doll heads.
1925 Robert Carl became sole owner.
1927 Manufactured dolls' heads, especially character dolls and babies.
1930 Still manufacturing dolls' heads.

P.M.
914
Germany

Trebor
Germany
22
P M

♡
PM
Herzi
Germany

Mark P.M. Dolls bearing this mark had been incorrectly identified until recently (when the Ciesliks of Germany published their identification books) as products of Otto Reincke.

The dolls' heads marked Trebor (Robert spelled backwards) were moulded by the owner Robert Carl. Most common mould numbers 914 and 22; other marks are Grete and Herzi. Robert Carl supplied heads to the firms of Carl Harmus and Gbr. Ohlhaver.

Porzellanfabrik Raunstein Raunstein, Germany 1892-1927+, porcelain factory

Although founded in 1783, there is no evidence for doll head manufacture before 1892.

1892 The factory was burnt down and then rebuilt. Production of doll heads.
1910 Produced character heads—mould numbers 5430 (stubborn), 5431 (laughing).
1918 Purchased doll factory of Amandus Michaelis.
1927 Dolls' heads, socket and shoulderplate, often of rather poor quality.

$$R - n$$

Mark Crossed flags, sometimes with R = n.

Putnam, Grace Storey USA 1922-25+

Copr by
J L Kallus
Germany
1394/3

Designed a doll's head that represented a three day old baby, which became the model for the famous Bye-Lo Baby. Grace Storey Putnam copyrighted her design in 1922. Manufacture of this popular doll's head continued for 20 years, during which time Bye-Los were manufactured with bisque, wax and composition heads, as well as in an all bisque version.

Porzellanfabrik Raunstein, crossed flags/B/No80. *Doreen Budd collection*

Mark Trebor Germany 22 P.6M

Rabery & Delphieu Paris, France 1856-98

R.4 D

1856 Firm was granted a patent for the use of pink cloth instead of kid for doll bodies.

1875 Advertised dolls with swivel or stationary heads on bodies of kid or linen.

1876 All kinds of jointed dolls, kid bodied dolls with bisque heads—swivel or stationary. Manufactured a large variety of marottes.

1878 Exhibited dressed and undressed dolls at the French Exposition.

1879 Dolls of all kinds and marottes with bisque heads were advertised.

1881 Bébés with wooden bodies, both dressed and undressed.

1883 Exhibited at the Amsterdam Exhibition where they won a silver medal.

1889 Rabery was awarded a silver medal at the Paris Exposition.

1890 Were using the initials R. D. for jointed Bébés.

1893 Exhibited at the Chicago World Fair.

1998-99 Genty succeeded Rabery & Delphieu, and was advertising walking Bébés bearing the trademark R. D. as listed by Dorothy Coleman.

1899 Genty became a founder of S.F.B.J.

The firm used both pressed and poured heads, and during the 1880s purchased bisque heads and arms from François Gaultier.

Mark RE/Nippon. *Hervey Bay, Queensland*

Raunstein see Porzellanfabrik Raunstein

RE Japan 1915-22 +

RE with crossed lines forming a diamond is a mark on many Japanese bisque headed dolls that are quite common in Australia. Made during the years of the First World War and after, because of their quality they could not compete when the full German production of dolls' heads began again in the early 1920s. Unfortunately the manufacturer who used this mark is as yet unknown.

Recknagel, Theodor Alexandrienthal, Germany, porcelain factory

121
R A
Germany

1886 The firm was founded by Theodor Recknagel.

1893 Took out a patent for dolls' heads (Mulattos) that could be made with coloured slip.

1894 Incorporated in the commercial register—production: bisque dolls' heads.

1897 Marks for Black and Mulatto heads were registered, and by the next year the factory was employing 200 workers.

1905 Expanded the factory.

1910 Registered six mould numbers for heads—226, 227, 1907, RI, RIV, RXII.

1912 Character doll head of porcelain with bonnet and cloth ribbon drawn through. Also registered eleven mould

All original clothes, 20 cm (8″), mark 24/Germany R14A. *Author's collection*

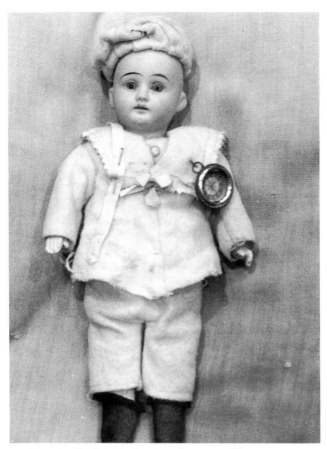

Recknagel, all original, sleeping glass eyes. *Ulverstone, Tasmania*

Recknagel R196A, cloth body, composition hands. *Private collection, Queensland*

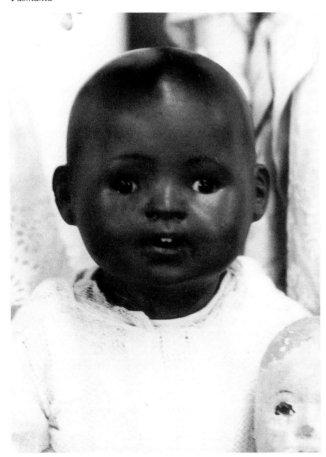

Recknagel. *Courtesy J. Brooks, Australian Doll Digest*

numbers: 22, 23, 24, 25, 26, 27, 28, 29, 30; also 31 for Max and 32 for Moritz.

1914 Registered 19 more numbers, for character dolls.

1930 The factory was still producing bisque dolls' heads. Dolls' heads have the letters R A on their heads, as well as numerals for the mould number.

Rohmer, Madame Marie Paris 1857–80

1857 Obtained two patents, one for a kid body with articulated joints, the other with stuffed arms.

1859–63 Advertised jointed dolls.

1867 Displayed dolls and jointed Bébés at the Paris Exposition.

1860–80s Sold jointed kid-body dolls and Bébés, as well as dressed Bébés.

Used swivel necks on shoulderplates made of china or bisque, and the dolls' heads could have glass eyes or painted eyes. One form of identification was the oval Rohmer stamp on the front of the body.

Royal Doulton

In the late 1970s and early 1980s the famous British porcelain manufacturer of figurines Royal Doulton made several bisque headed dolls under licence to Peggy Nesbit, the well known English character dollmaker. These dolls included an 8″ (20 cm) model or doll of Queen Elizabeth in Jubilee regalia. Child dolls with bisque heads representing the Royal children were also made. In the early 1980s they made a series of dolls designed to represent the old rhyme about birthdays—Monday's Child, Saturday's Child etc.

S & Q see Schuetzmeister & Quendt.

Scherf, Peter Sonneberg, Germany 1883-1927, doll factory
1883 Was incorporated in the commercial register.
1890-1909 Made and exported inexpensive dolls.
1916 Advertised character dolls with the mould numbers 100, 101, 102, 103 and registered the trademark The Fairy Kid.
1924 Referred to as an exporter of dolls.
1926-27 Dolls, baby dolls in chemises or fully dressed were advertised.

Dolls can have mould numbers 1899, 1901, 1902, as well as the A.M. trademark of Armand Marseille along with the P.Sch marking of Peter Sherf.

Schmidt, Bruno Walterhausen 1900-30, doll factory
1900 Bruno Schmidt founded a doll factory, with the heads being supplied by Bahr & Proschild.
1903 Bisque headed ball jointed dolls of various qualities and stiff jointed dolls were advertised.
1904 Registered the letters B S W with a heart (Herz).
1918 Bought the porcelain factory of Bahr & Proschild, which made bisque dolls and heads.
1921 Doll factory was producing first class jointed dolls, finest character bent limb babies and toddlers. The Herz (heart) trade mark can be found with or without the letters B S W.

1925 Still advertising dolls.
1930 Produced dolls with bisque heads on toddler type bodies that could sit and also stand.
Character babies—mould numbers 2048, 2094, 2096, 2097.
All bisque baby—mould number 425.

Schmidt, Franz Georgenthal 1890-1937, doll factory

1890 Factory founded by Franz Schmidt (owner), who once worked for J.D. Kestner, and Traugott Schmidt (sculptor).
1891 One year later advertised ball jointed dolls of fine and average quality with bisque heads. Early trademark— an anvil, also S.&C., sometimes with Simon & Halbig.
1898 Advertised that the doll factory was powered by steam and producing ball jointed dolls, stiff jointed dolls,

Royal Doulton, Saturday's Child

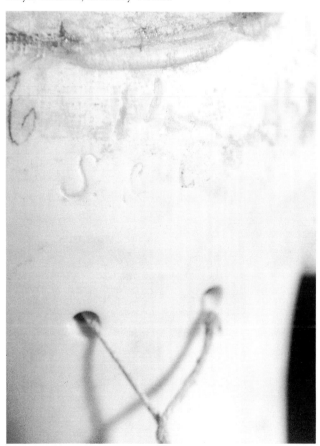

Franz Schmidt head showing holes and string used to tie back eye weight during transportation. c. 1893

Franz Schmidt, mark 14/ S & C. *Kempsey*

Mark F.S&C 1278/28/Deponiert. *Private collection, Queensland*

shoulderheads of bisque, and spare parts—arms, legs, bodies, socket heads etc.

1902 Registered trade mark F.S. & Co. with a doll and crossed hammers.

1906 Sold fine ball jointed dolls and spare parts and dolls' heads of all kinds.

1912 Applied for a patent for pierced nostrils in a doll's head.

1913 Applied for a patent for a moving tongue in a doll's head, and advertised 120 styles of dolls in their babies series.

1914 The factory was the first doll factory to produce character babies with sleeping eyes. This invention was copied by the other doll companies.

1921 Manufactured bent limb baby bodies, toddlers, and ball jointed dolls.

1937 Went into bankruptcy.

Many important inventions pertaining to doll manufacture can be attributed to Franz Schmidt. 1912—open nostrils in doll heads. 1913—moveable tongue in a doll head. 1914—universal joints. 1928—eye bars for doll heads. His bisque dolls' heads were mainly made by Simon & Halbig. The small 'z' on some of his heads indicates the approximate size in centimetres of the doll for which the dolls' head was made.

Mould numbers for Character babies were: 1272, 1286, 1295, 1296, 1297, 1310.

Schmitt & Fils (Son) Paris, dollmakers

1877 Maurice and Charles Schmitt were granted a French patent for decorating shoulderheads for dolls and Bébés. This improved method would permit desired shades and colours to be applied to bisque dolls' heads.

1878 Awarded a silver medal at the Paris Exposition for their dolls and Bébés with bisque heads.

1883 Experimented, and covered some of the bisque heads in wax to give them an improved appearance.

1879-90 Advertised their speciality to be an indestructible jointed Bébé called Bébé Schmitt. The doll was exported as well as being sold on the French market.

All the known heads on these dolls have so far been proved to have been made in the pressed bisque style.

Schoenau, Arthur Sonneberg, Germany 1884–1930, doll factory

See also Schoenau & Hoffmeister

The history of the two firms is intertwined as Arthur Schoenau was the founder of both companies. He used the trademark AS or ASS.

1884 The firm Arthur Schoenau was incorporated in the commercial register.

1901 Porcelain factory of Schoenau & Hoffmeister, Burggrub was founded by Arthur Schoenau and Carl Hoffmeister, both of Sonneberg.

1907 Difference of opinion between Arthur Schoenau, who preferred socket heads, and Carl Hoffmeister, who insisted on shoulderplate heads.

1911 After Arthur Schoenau died his two sons split the estate, with Curt taking over the doll factory (Arthur Schoenau) and Hans the porcelain factory (Schoenau & Hoffmeister).

1920 The doll Hanna was advertised, as well as the fact that the firm was manufacturing heads.

1930s Export business intensified.

When Carl Schoenau returned from England in the 1930s he brought with him a postcard with a portrait of Princess Elizabeth of England on it. This was to be the model for Casar Schneider, who sculpted the head of a doll called Princess Elizabeth.

It is interesting that although the firm of Schoenau & Hoffmeister was a porcelain factory, according to the Ciesliks, the company of Arthur Schoenau was supplied with dolls' heads by Simon & Halbig, Gbr. Kuhnlenz, Theodor Recknagel, Gbr. Beck, Carl Muller and Bahr & Proschild, and doll bodies were bought from H. Ring & Co. Until 1930 these heads were supplied marked Porzellanfabrik Burggrub *without the star*. The mould number 1900 can be marked AS DEP.

Schoenau & Hoffmeister Porzellanfabrik Burggrub, Burggrub, Germany, porcelain manufacturer

1901 Company was founded by Arthur Schoenau and Carl Hoffmeister.

1909 Due to a difference of opinion over the heads to be manufactured Carl Hoffmeister (who insisted on shoulderheads) left the company. Arthur Schoenau continued with his socket heads.

1911 With the death of Arthur Schoenau, his son Hans took over as director.

1914 Hans Schoenau died. His mother and his brother Curt (Arthur Schoenau) ran the company.

1927 Baby shoulderheads (flange necks) and new born babies were advertised.

1930 Reference to dolls' heads, baby dolls and shoulderheads.

1938 Still supplying dolls' heads to Cuno & Otto Dressel, Gbr. Eckhardt, E. Maar & Sohn, Herman von Berg and others.

Porzellanfabrik
Bürggrub

Princess Elizabeth

Madein Germany

Made in Germany
S ⭐ H
N. K.B.

S ⭐ H
4000·9

S ⭐ H
1909

Germany

Beautiful new born baby doll heads have the letters S H P B, the star and the letters N K B and/or W S B. Mould numbers 900 and 1914; 70, 169, 1800, 1904, 1906, 1909, 1916, 1923.

Mould numbers for Character babies 169, 769.

Head markings: Arthur Schoenau—AS or ASS.

Schoenau & Hoffmeister—SHPB with a 5 pointed star; Schoenau & Hoffmeister, Porzellanfabrik Burggrub.

The five pointed star with the letters SHPB was used until 1930, after which the heads were marked Porzellanfabrik Burggrub.

F.S. & Co 1272/32Z. Deponiert. *Lesley Hurford collection*

This doll is thought to have been saved from the shipwreck of the *Yungala* early this century, mark SPBH. *Private collection, Queensland*

66 cm (26″), mark SPBH/1909–6

Shoulderplate, kid body,
mark 2000/SPBH/2

Walker with metal hinges for knee joints,
mark Germany/SPBH/914/72

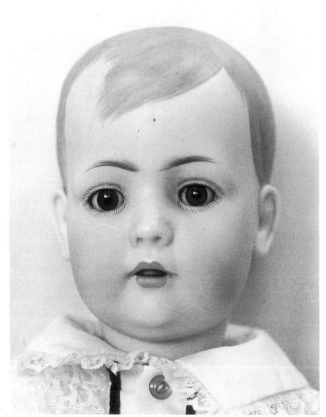

Bruno Schmidt 2048/5. *Private collecton, Queensland*

Schmitt & Fils, France. *Lesley Hurfood collection*

Schutzmeister & Quendt Germany 1889–1920 + , porcelain factory

1889 Porcelain factory was founded by Wilhelm Quendt and Philipp Schutzmeister and bisque dolls' heads were produced.

1893 Showed fine bisque dolls' heads and porcelain heads at the World Exhibition, Chicago.

1908 Schutzmeister became sole owner after Quendt left the company.

1918 Company bought by the large Bing concern and thereafter produced dolls' heads only for doll factories associated with Bing, namely Welsch & Co., and Kammer & Reinhardt.

1920 Manufactured bisque dolls, doll heads and jointed porcelain dolls.

1927 Tea-cosy dolls, half dolls, doll heads.

1930 With a staff of 70 manufactured porcelain dolls, tea-cosy dolls, half dolls, dolls' heads.

Mark S and Q entwined.
Mould numbers 101, 02, 1376; babies 201, 204, 300, 301; black baby 252.

Seyfarth & Reinhardt Walterhausen, Germany 1922–30 + , doll factory

1922 After leaving Gans & Seyfarth, Hugo Seyfarth joined with Hugo Reinhardt to found Seyfarth & Reinhardt.

1923 Manufactured ball jointed dolls, used Ernst Heubach heads especially 312. Trademark SUR registered. Exported dolls.

1925 Ma-ma dolls with bisque heads, baby dolls, jointed dolls, dolls that could sit and stand.

1926 Dolls were distributed through Louis Wolf & Co.

1927 Obtained a patent for 'living eyes'. These eyes were used by both Alt, Beck & Gottschalck and Koenig & Wernicke. Advertised dolls with bisque heads on cloth bodies, also jointed dolls and bent limb babies.

S.F.B.J. (Société Française de Fabrication de Bébés et Jouets) France 1899–1950s

DÉPOSE   S.F.B.J.   S.F.B.J.   SFBJ
S.F.B.J.   60   236   230
          PARIS   PARIS   PARIS

From the mid 1890s to 1899 competition from German manufacturers had increased immensely, and they were difficult years for most French doll companies. The Société Française de Fabrication de Bébés et Jouets (French Society of Manufacturers of Dolls and Toys) was formed. This amalgamation of companies consisted of Jumeau (1320 shares), Fleischmann (1000) and Bloedel (1000), Bouchet

Schutzmeister & Quendt mark Sand Q Superimposed 201

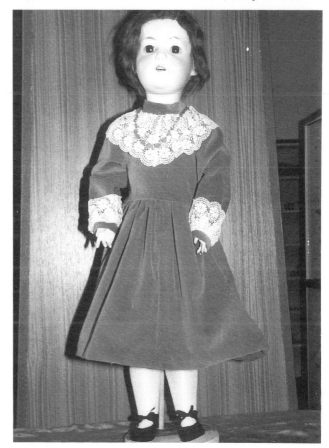

Seyfarth & Reinhardt, head by Ernst Heubach, mark Heubach Koppelsdorf/312/SUR

Sleeping glass eyes, mark S.F.B.J./60/PARIS

Painted eyes, original clothes, 18 cm (7″), mark S.F.B.J./60/PARIS. *Sydney*

Mark S.F.B.J./235/PARIS. *Lesley Hurford collection*

Mark S.F.B.J./227/PARIS. *Lesley Hurford collection*

(200), Genty (110), Girard (Bru) (110), Remignard (100), Gobert (80), Gaultier (100), Werthheimer (50), Pintel (400).

1900 Dolls of all types from poupards to dressed Bébés, totalling up to 15,000 dolls per day, were manufactured. Two hundred different moulds, including heads, arms and legs, were used each day, which kept 2000 people employed.

Emile Jumeau supplied S.F.B.J. with the bulk of his models, trademarks and materials. Because of this his name was used on dolls for many years. The Bébés made by S.F.B.J. in the early years are hard to distinguish from those made by Jumeau before the amalgamation.

Because of the great demand for their product S.F.B.J. were forced to look further afield for someone to meet their demands at a realistic price. Because of Fleischmann's connection with Germany it was possible for them to import large quantities of German heads, with Simon & Halbig being the main supplier. These heads usually bore the letters DEP and one of the following mould numbers: 1039, 1078 or 1079 as well as the letters S & H or the whole name. These mould numbers were not entirely reserved for S.F.B.J. as other German and French manufacturers also used these heads, including Decamps who used the heads with mould numbers 1039 and 1079.

Other heads manufactured in Germany and stamped DEP may also bear a red stamp with the words Tête Jumeau; there are two kinds of Tête Jumeau stamps—the blurred coral red or the clear and bold stamp in garnet red. The main identification of the dolls' origin relies on the S.F.B.J. bodies, which differ from those made in Germany. Even though made in Germany these DEP heads are of a high quality and sought after by collectors.

Whereas S.F.B.J. used many of the Jumeau moulds, they only used two of Bru's ideas. One was Girard's 1897 patent for a mechanical walker and the other was the nursing Bébé (Bébé Téteur), but in the early years of S.F.B.J. a Jumeau body was used on the Bébé Téteur. Later S.F.B.J. manufactured their own special model, mould number 242.

1905 Registered the S.F.B.J. trademark.

Began to make Bluette, a doll that remained popular for 60 years.

Bluette was a small articiulated Bébé with a bisque head that measured 27 cm (10½″) tall. Starting in 1933 she was 29 cm (11½″) tall. Originally given free by *La Semaine de Suzette*, a weekly magazine for girls, the doll had to be inexpensive. It had to be easy to dress, hence the jointed body. To keep expenses down, an existing open mouth Jumeau head mould was used, and originally the eyes were fixed blue ones. She was made to use dress patterns published to help young girls to learn how to sew.

In the beginning the heads were not marked S.F.B.J., and it was not until later that the numbers 301, 60 or the mark Unis were used.

The Character Bébés of S.F.B.J. were their most original product and the main item manufactured. From 1910 until World War II they did not stop creating head moulds. Their Character Bébés were very realistic and lifelike and all models were sculpted by artists, including Poulbot and Lejieune.

1916 S.F.B.J. dolls dressed as soldiers were advertised.

All original, 15 cm (6″), mark S.F.B.J./60/PARIS. *Private collection, Queensland*

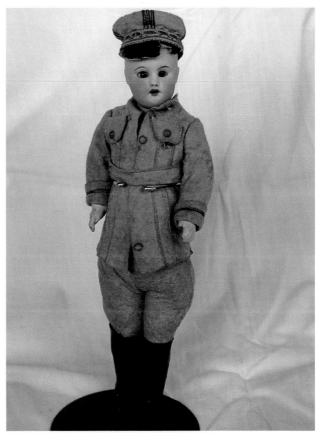

General Joffre. All original, simple straight body, legs and arms, S.F.B.J. 60. *Private collection, Brisbane*

Pair of S.F.B.J.-60 twins, 60 cm (24″). *Private collection, Brisbane*

1920s Unis trademark was registered. Unis France was only used after 1924, sometimes with mould numbers such as 301 or 60 underneath.

1922 S.F.B.J. owned four factories and advertised Bébé Bru and Bébé Jumeau.

1924 S.F.B.J. had become an entirely French firm employing 250 personnel in the office and 1000 men and women workers. Between 11,000 and 12,000 dolls per day were manufactured. The articulated dolls had 11 pieces and the non-articulated dolls 5 pieces. Covering a wide range of designs, four million dolls were produced each year.

1925 Decorative Arts Grand Prize was won for Bébés and dolls at the Paris Exposition of Decorative Arts.

1928 Bébé Bru, Bébé Jumeau, Eden Bébé were among the tradenames advertised, as well as Esquimaux dolls and silent or talking poupards. Produced Bambino, the baby brother doll of Bluette.

1931 Won a prize at the Colonial Exposition in Paris. Among the collection were several exotic creations including Bamboula, the small black brother of Bambino.

1938 The Princess dolls were produced; the first were given to the two English Princesses, Princess Elizabeth and Princess Margaret Rose. They were made with a complete wardrobe of clothes. Mould number 306 was later produced for sale as Marianne, a blonde haired doll, and France, who was a brown eyed brunette doll.

Continued manufacturing dolls after World War II, but couldn't compete with foreign companies, mainly American, so in 1957 doll activity came to a halt.

Mark S.F.B.J./223. *Lesley Hurford collection*

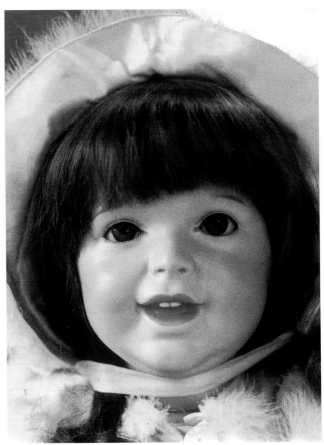

Commonly called 'Laughing Jumeau', 66 cm (26″), mark S.F.B.J. 236. *Private collection, Queensland*

The grandson of Paul Girand, (of Bru) André, was one of the last directors of S.F.B.J., resigning in 1958.

In 1963 S.F.B.J. completely modified their factory to manufacture ball point pens.

Over the years of operation S.F.B.J. used several different marks:

1. S.F.B.J. in quite large letters stamped in a hollow in a horizontal line, found mainly on dolls' heads attached to walking dolls with patented mechanism—circa 1905.

2. S.F.B.J. in a hollow circle, quartered, with a letter in each quarter. This trademark was registered in England and was found on Bébés early this century.

3. An incised S.F.B.J. Paris with a number representing the mould in the middle. Number lower down on the nape of the neck indicates the head size. Another number may be present near the cut out (usually found on dolls manufactured after 1920) which will be the year of manufacture.

4. Unis France only used after 1924, sometimes with numbers 301 or 60 underneath. The extra numbers to be found at the sides of the Unis France mark are, on the left the Trade Union number, and on the right the Chamber Syndicate number (S.F.B.J.'s was 149—which had been Girard's before). S.F.B.J. always used its own personal mark on Character Bébé heads.

Shoulderplate head (shoulderhead)

The name shoulderplate or shoulderhead is normally used for the type of doll's head found on a kid, Kidlyn, or cloth body. It is a one piece head with a wide chest piece which fitted over the shoulder section of the doll's torso.

Nearly all the early untinted bisque heads (parian) were shoulderplate heads. Some of the early Fashion dolls had socket heads attached to separate chest pieces (see swivel heads).

The shoulderplate head often had the shoulder section attached by glue and reinforced by stitching strong fibrous thread through the holes at the bottom of the shoulderplate. Another method found in older dolls with kid bodies involved attaching the head to the course cotton underbody or even directly to the straw stuffing. The kid outer covering was then mounted firmly over the shoulderplate and glued into place, thus keeping the head held firmly in position. This method often hides the essential information needed to identify a doll's origin.

The favoured shoulderplate dolls with turned heads were made by cutting the original clay model at the neck. It was then remounted again, slightly inclined to suit and smoothed at the seams, before another mould was made. In this way several variations could be made from a single clay model.

Simon & Halbig Grafenhain, Germany 1870-1930 + , porcelain factory

1078
S & H
Germany

D E P
S H
Germany

S&H 1009
DEP
Germany

SH 1039
DEP

1299
SIMON & HALBIG

The firm of Simon and Halbig was the second largest German manufacturer of dolls' heads. They did not make doll bodies, except for the all bisque dolls. Many new

Mark S.F.B.J./252/PARIS. *Commonly called 'Pouty'. Lesley Hurford collection*

Shoulderplate under body. Body has Ne Plus Ultra joint at hips. *Courtesy Doll & Toy Collection, Brisbane*

collectors are unaware that Simon and Halbig made heads for many of the famous German doll factories, including Kammer & Reinhardt, and also for French companies such as Jumeau and S.F.B.J.

1870 Manufactured shoulderplate heads with artistically modelled hair and ribbons, with or without glass eyes.

1879 A registration of design patent and number series for doll heads was taken out by Wilhelm Simon and Carl Halbig.

1887 Registered the brand DEP or 'dep', and all heads, especially mould number 968, should be thus marked. At the same time a double-faced doll was registered—one a laughing face, the other crying.

1893 Produced bisque heads, bathing dolls, doll bodies; exported bathing dolls and doll heads. Had sample stores at Hamburg, Amsterdam, Paris and Buenos Aires.

1894 Wilhelm Simon died.

1895 Carl Halbig took over.

1898 At the State Trade Exhibition, Gotha, the firm received an honorable citation for 'dolls' heads, perfectly modelled and manufactured'.

1905 S & H trademark was registered for 'dollheads and bathing dolls'.

1909 Character heads in the 100 series went into production for Kammer & Reinhardt.

1913 Six kilns and 220 workers were kept busy producing doll heads and bathing dolls.

1919 Carl Halbig (80 years old) celebrated the 50th anniversary of the firm.

1920 Kammer & Reinhardt became sole owner, had four kilns operating and employed 100 workers. Manufactured bisque heads, all bisque dolls and composition heads.

1930 Bisque heads were still produced and exported to all countries.

According to extensive research carried out by the Ciesliks on German doll manufacturers, Simon & Halbig supplied the following doll factories with bisque dolls' heads. Where known, the mould number supplied to each factory is also given.

C.M. Bergmann, Walterhausen, Eleonore and Columbia mould no. 1280, also mould nos 612, 615, 1279.

Carl Bergner, Sonneberg double and multi-face dolls' heads.

Cuno & Otto Dressel, Sonneberg, Jutta dolls' heads mould nos 1348, 1349, 1848, 1849, 1912, 1914, 1920; Flapper doll head mould no. 1468, 1469; also 1049.

Edison Phonograph doll Mould nos 719 and 917.

R. Eeckhoff, Gronigen (Holland)

Fleischmann & Bloedel, Furth, heads marked DEP for French market.

Hamburger & Co., Berlin, Imperial mould no. 1250, and Santa mould nos 1249 and 1429.

Heinrich Handwerck, Walterhausen, mould nos 160, 530, 540, 550, 927, 159.

Adolf Hulss, Walterhausen, mould nos 156 and 176.

Emile Jumeau, Paris, mould nos 1019, 1039, 1079, 1159, and the number series 200.

Kammer & Reinhardt, Walterhausen, all doll heads from 1902 onwards. Most of the K * R character heads carry both sets of initials or names.

Mark S & H 1248. *Melbourne*

Mark 1079 S&H 9½

K * R Simon & Halbig 403

66 cm (26″), mark SIMON & Halbig/K * R/66

Uncle Sam for Cuno & Otto Dressel. *Courtesy Billie Nelson Tyrell, USA*

Louis Lindner & Sohne Mould no. 1339.

Roullet & Decamp, Paris Ondine mould nos 1039, 1079, and mould no. 1019.

Franz Schmidt, Georgenthal Mould no. 1180 plus S & C, also 1293, 1295, 1296, 1297, 1298, 1299, 1310.

S.F.B.J., Paris (France) From 1900 to 1914 mould nos 1039 and 1079.

Carl Trautmann, Finsterbergen

Welsch & Co., Sonneberg

Hugo Wiegard, Walterhausen Mould no. 1351.

Wagner & Zetzsche Mould no. 949.

Weisenthal, Schindel & Kallenberg, Walterhausen Mould no. 541.

Adolf Wislizenus, Walterhausen Old Glory.

Simon & Halbig, beside making dolls' heads in the accepted colour, made exotics and other specialities.

Belton heads   Mould nos 719, 740, 949

Gibson Girl   Mould no. 1159

Googly   Mould no. 1340

All bisque   Mould nos 837, 886

Black dolls' heads   Mould nos 739, 759, 769, 1009, 1248, 1301, 1302, 1358, 1368

Oriental dolls' heads   Mould nos 607, 1098, 1099, 1129, 1199, 1329

1299 Simon & Halbig. *Private collection, Queensland*

Mark Simon & Halbig 171. *Lesley Hurford collection*

Mark S & H 1078. *Private collection, Queensland*

You may wonder why there are so many of the four figure mould numbers ending in the same numerals. Simon & Halbig had a system whereby you can usually identify the type of head the doll has.

Ending with 8: the beginning of a series, model head—example 1078
Ending with 9: styled as a socket head—example 1079
Ending with 0: styled as a shoulderplate head
Ending with 1: styled as a swivel head–shoulderplate

Simon & Halbig also used the 800 series on bathing dolls and small dolls. The small dolls or even dolls'-house dolls have long moulded stockings and shoes and range in size from 15–21 cm (6–8 in), are either unmarked or have S & H with numbers such as 837, 852, 878, 880, 881, 886, 887, 890.

The list of mould numbers used by Simon & Halbig for their own personal production is just too large to record in this book, as practically every type of bisque doll's head has been found with an S & H mark: dolls' heads with modelled, moulded hair or wigs, Belton type heads; with stationary or sleeping glass eyes, painted eyes, flirty eyes; closed mouth, open–closed mouth or open mouth with teeth; and with or without pierced ears (most 19th and early 20th century dolls' heads had pierced ears).

Snow Babies 1910–28 +

These are small, normally one piece, all bisque, statue-like dolls with a pebbly finish made of ground porcelain covering their moulded snow suits. Some only have this special finish on head hoods, others have everything covered except the face and hands. These delightful small character dolls can be found as just a one piece doll or a doll with cast skis or a doll or dolls with cast on sled, and in other configurations. Some were used as cake decorations and also as Christmas decorations.

Made by Bahr & Proschild, Hertwig, C.F. Kling, Kley and Hahn. The name is a reference to Peary's daughter who was photographed bundled in a snow suit. (Peary's party was the first to reach the North Pole.)

Snow Babies. All bisque covered in ground bisque granules. *Private collection, Brisbane*

Socket head

This type of bisque head was mainly used on jointed dolls and baby dolls with bodies made of composition or a mixture of composition and wood. The bottom of the doll's head was hemispherical in shape and fitted snugly and smoothly into the neck socket on composition bodies, or the shoulder section of a swivel head. The bisque head was often connected to the body by means of a head button placed inside the head, that was then attached to the body with rubber cord, wire and rubber, springs, or a combination of these. In most cases the head of a Jumeau doll had a special spring toggle inside the head which was attached by rubber cord to the legs etc.

Early socket heads referred to as Belton heads had no pate opening. There are a variety of cuts to form open socket heads: the high cut favoured by most German manufacturers, the low cut towards the nape of the head used by the French. Most German heads also had a flange or lip pointing inwards at the top of the open cut, whereas most French manufactured heads in the early years had no lip at the top at all. These open cut socket heads allowed for easy installation of eyes etc. The hole in the top of the head was closed by a pate of cork, wood, plaster or concavely pressed cardboard to which the wig was attached. Many baby heads are referred to as dome socket heads. This means that the top of the head is closed and often the dome head has finely moulded hair detail that is then painted.

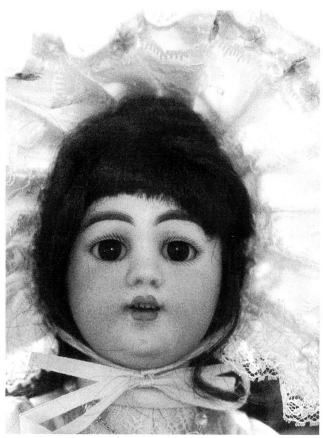

Simon & Halbig 1009/D. *Private collection, Taree, NSW*

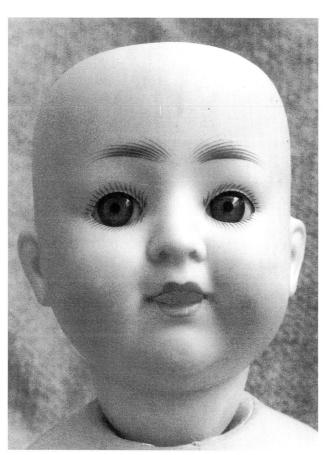

Two all bisque dolls, 80 yrs old. Notice five cent piece. Numbers 228? on backs. *Private collection, Sunshine Coast*

Socket head, mark Porzellanfabrik-Burggrub/169/3. *Courtesy Discovery Corner, Brisbane*

Erste Steinbacher, Porzellanfabrik, original clothes, mark E.
St. P./23/9½. *Private collection, Tasmania*

Edmund Ulrich Steiner. Notice sheen on eyebrows. Kid
body, mark E.U.St in a diamond

Special—Spezial

Some controversy still exists over these two ways of spelling
the name. One school of thought is that Special was on dolls
sold to the English speaking market, whereas Spezial was
for sale on the European market. Certain known dolls have
been found with one or the other spelling.

Special: Armand Marseille; Schoenau & Hoffmeister and
Adolf Wislizenus have all used dolls' heads with Special
on them.

Spezial: Used by Charles M. Bergmann on a bisque head
on a composition body, circa 1910. According to research
by the Ciesliks, a line of dolls by Franz Kuhles had this
name. Kley & Hahn are reported to have used Spezial
for their German speaking customers and Special for their
English speaking customers.

Steiner, August Koppelsdorf, Germany, doll factory
1912 Bought the factory of Heinrich Steiner.
1923 Enlarged factory.
1938 Factory still existed.
Marks Dolls' heads have A.S. Germany and numbers.

Steiner, Edmund Ulrich Sonneberg, Germany 1902–16,
doll factory

1902 Registered trademark and business which was
described as the production and supply of dolls.
A shoulderplate with the initials E.U.St is known to have
a body with a sticker on it saying American Beauty.

Steiner, Hermann Tann Rhon, Sonneberg, Germany
1911–30, porcelain and doll factory
1920 A porcelain factory was opened with 300 workers.
Advertised jointed dolls and dressed dolls.
1926 Advertised 'special factory for all kinds of dolls' heads,
newborn babies, baby heads, character heads, socket
heads'. Hermann Steiner was the sole owner and the firm
was called Porzellanfabrik Hermann Steiner.
1927 Manufactured bisque socket heads, baby heads,
Character heads, heads of Mulattos, heads of Blacks (with
or without sleeping eyes), bathing dolls and their
speciality, newborn baby dolls.

$$\boxed{\dfrac{S}{H}}\ N \qquad \begin{array}{c}\textit{Made in}\\ \textit{Germany}\end{array} \qquad \begin{array}{c}12\ 8\\ Herm\ Steiner\end{array} \qquad \begin{array}{c}Germany\\ 2\ 47\end{array}$$

Mark Most common H with S across the bar of the H.
Mould numbers 128, 133 (googly), 134 (black), 240
(newborn), 245 (baby), 401 (shoulderplate).
Several years ago a doll came to me for identification. It
had exactly the same mark as a German Hermann Steiner,
the H with the S through the bar, but under the H and
S was the word NIPPON. Quite an enigma; was this head
made in Japan before being made up in Germany or was
it an early 1920s copy of the German doll?

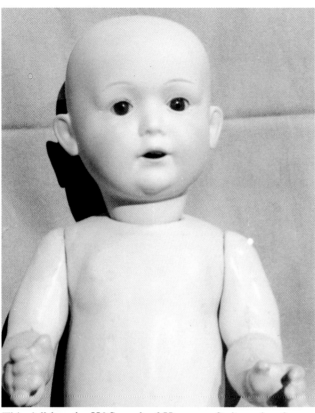

This doll has the H&S mark of Hermann Steiner plus the word NIPPON

Steiner, Jules Nicholas Paris 1855–91, 1892 Amadée Lafosse, 1893–98 Widow Lafosse, 1899–1901 Jules Mettais, 1904–08 Edmond Daspres

Jules Nicolas Steiner was a clockmaker by trade, which may explain why there were so many mechanical dolls produced by the firm.

STEINER   **11**   J.STEINER
S.G.D.G.   Sᵀᴱ S.G.D.G.
PARIS   PARIS   PARIS

1855 The firm was founded by Jules Steiner, who was the brains behind this successful French dollmaking firm until 1891. It was during his years with the firm that some of the best loved French dolls were manufactured, especially the A mould Steiners.

1865 Bébés, dolls, talking dolls and mechanical dolls were advertised.

1870 Produced a walking Steiner that had wheels under the feet. The doll had a bisque head with an open mouth and bisque arms.

1889 Awarded a gold medal for his exhibit at the Paris Exhibition.

1890 Received the Diplome d'Honneur at the Paris Exposition.

Applied for a French patent for walking dolls with clockwork mechanism. The dolls were named Bébé Premier Pas and Bébé Marcheur. The instructions for these mechanical walking Steiners were in four languages—French, English, German and Spanish.

Jules Steiner. *Courtesy Jacki Brooks, Quaint Collectables, Goulburn, NSW*

Jules Steiner. *Private collection, Armidale*

1891 Honored with Hors Concours for an exhibit at the Paris Exposition. This was the end of the Jules Steiner era.

1892 Amadée Lafosse became head of the firm. Advertised that the firm owned 24 patents for dolls and produced five categories of Bébés—talking and ordinary, sleeping eyes, jointed wrists, mechanical and walking. These Bébés had thick or heavy bisque heads which were referred to in advertising as 'unbreakable'.

1894 Widow Lafosse had taken over the firm and by 1895 was using the Bébé Phénix trademark.

1897 Obtained a French patent for a talking, kiss throwing doll. Advertised that the Steiner firm owned thirty patents.

1899 Widow Lafosse was succeeded by Jules Mettais, who registered three new trademarks.

1900 An advertisement stated that the Steiner firm, besides making five categories of dolls (as they did in 1892), were manufacturing Negro and Mulatto Bébés. As the 1900 Paris Exposition Jules Mettais won a silver medal for his exhibit.

1901 Used the trade name Mascotte from the May Frères (Bros) company.

1906 Edmond Daspres was listed as the head of the Steiner firm.

The firm of Steiner had four different heads of firm in less than fifteen years from 1891, and this is the reason why there is such a variety of trademarks and marks found on dolls' heads attributed to the firm of Jules Steiner.

Stone bisque

This is the name given to a poor quality, rather porous bisque with an overall off-white tinge. Many Japanese one piece dolls and small dolls were made of this bisque. This type of doll sold quite cheaply on the Australian market between World War I and World War II, often imitating European produced dolls, but of much poorer quality. Some of these dolls were produced in occupied Japan after World War II.

W&S, Walther & Sohn

Stone bisque babies in original blanket that was pocketed to take them. *Private collection, Devonport, Tasmania*

Stone bisque, all original. *Private collection, Queensland*

Jules Steiner. *Courtesy Jacki Brooks, Australian Doll Digest*

Storybook Dolls California, USA 1941-50 +

Nancy Ann or Storybook Dolls were first manufactured by Nancy Ann Abbott in 1941.

In the early years, Miss Abbott bought her small all bisque doll bodies from Europe and Japan and repainted them in her factory in the USA. Unfortunately 50-60% of them proved to be defective, so she and her partner, A.L. Rowland, imported clays from England and began manufacturing their own dolls. World War II made materials hard to get, so she dipped the dolls' feet into black paint to represent shoes.

Made in two sizes 5″ (12.5 cm) and 6½″ (16.5 cm), these small all bisque dolls were dressed as famous nursery rhyme and fairytale characters.

The bisque dolls were superseded by hard plastic dolls in the early 1950s.

Strobel & Wilken Co. Cincinnatti, Ohio, USA and Sonneberg, Germany, importers and agents

The firm of Strobel & Wilken imported many different German and Japanese dolls from 1881 until 1923 when the American business was liquidated.

The firm then re-establishd itself in Sonneberg, Germany and became agents for many dolls, both American and

Storybook Dolls. One on left, hard plastic, sleeping eyes, after 1950s. Doll on right, bisque, painted eyes, before 1950s.
Private collection, Devonport, Tasmania

Storybook Doll. All bisque, jointed doll, all original. *Private collection, Brisbane*

Unis France/306/Jumeau 'Princess Elizabeth'
Private collection, Queensland

German, and imported into Germany the American made Schoenut.

Up until recently, the entwined mark of S and W has been mistakenly accredited to Strobel & Wilken, when it actually belonged to Walther & Sohn, Germany.

Swaine & Co. Huttensteinach, Germany 1910-23, porcelain factory

1856 William Swaine was the sole owner, but was not then making dolls.
1910 Were known to be manufacturing character dolls' heads, including the dome headed Lori. Displayed character doll heads at the Leipzig Fair.
1914 William Swaine died.
1917 New owners, and in 1923 firm became Gbr. Schoenau, Swaine & Co.

Only produced dolls' heads for a short time, and these heads are stamped with a green circle on the back.

Tiny Babe see Horsman, E.I.

Trebor see Porzellanfabrik Mengersgereuth

Unis France France 1922-40s
Many of the smaller dolls manufactured by S.F.B.J. after 1922 were marked with the Unis France trademark, particu-

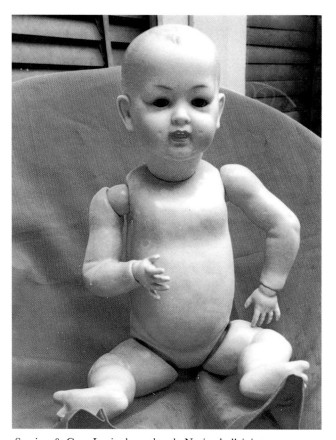

Swaine & Co., Lori, dome head. Notice ball joint at shoulder, on a bent limb body

Two Unis France dolls, composition bodies, painted eyes, dressed in original French provincial costume, PARIS/UNIS FRANCE/301. *Author's collection*

J.L. Verlingue, France

larly those that were sold as souvenir dolls in ethnic costume. Unis stands for Union Nationale Inter-Syndicale.

Mould numbers 60 and 301, both for normal heads, can be found along with the Unis France markings.

71 (UNIS FRANCE) 149
301

Probably the most famous doll of all to bear the Unis France mark is mould number 306 in conjunction with the word Jumeau, found on what is known as the Princess Elizabeth doll.

Verlingue J. Boulogne-sur-Mer and Montreuil-sous-Bois, France 1915–21 +

PETITE FRANCIASE
FRANCE
JV
LIANE

Although quite a few dolls are found in Australia with the Verlingue mark, that of an anchor and JV, very little is known about the manufacturer of these bisque dolls' heads. A 1920 listing for H. Delcourt, includes JV and Petite Française as part of his trademarks. It is known that H. Delcourt was the successor to Gesland.

In 1921 Verlingue had a factory at Boulogne, Paris and the address and telephone number were the same as those of Gesland.

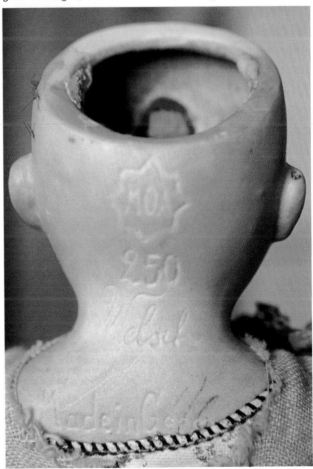

Shoulderplate, kid body. Notice original price in pencil 1/6d, mark MOA/Welsch/250/

W see also Walterhausen Puppenfabrik

The initial W is often found in the middle of a bisque doll's forehead, just below the pate mounting. It is found on Kammer & Reinhardt–Simon & Halbig dolls and Heinrich Handwerck marked dolls, and as all these were manufactured in the Walterhausen Puppenfabrik, this W is associated with the firm as a marking.

Wagner & Zetsche Ilmenau, Germany 1886–1930 + , doll factory

1886 Took out registrations for doll bodies and doll shoes. The marked kid bodies made by Wagner & Zetsche in their early years had very fine quality bisque or china heads marked on the back with three or four digit mould numbers, many of which could be those of Alt, Beck and Gottschalck.

1888 Used Simon & Halbig mould 949 on some of their bodies.

1891–97 Produced doll bodies of cloth and leather, and dolls which were sold in Europe, North America and Australia.

1907 A body of imitation leather was developed.

1910 A special leathering coated body for character dolls was developed with moveable hips, and by 1911 this body had been adapted so that a character doll could sit like a bent limb baby doll.

1910–16 Most of the bisque heads used were bought from Gbr. Heubach.

1916–30 Mostly composition heads were used.

1938 Still listed as manufacturing leather bodies for dolls.

Walking dolls

Most of the so-called walking dolls of the 19th century were propelled by means of a clockwork mechanism in one way or another. The Autoperipatekos by Enoch Rice Morrison was probably the most famous of all.

In 1870 Jules Steiner produced a doll that had wheels under its feet, and by the use of a clockwork mechanism was able to walk.

Claude Joseph Simonot of Paris registered a design in 1892/3 for a doll that could turn its head as it walked without using a clockwork mechanism.

Fleischmann & Bloedel were assigned the rights to use this patent, and within a few years many other companies took out patents or made similar walking dolls. Among these companies were Roullet & Decamps, Rabery & Delphieu and Edmund Ulrich Steiner.

Shortly after World War I another innovation in walking dolls was introduced. It was the cloth bodied Ma-ma doll with swinging legs, that could 'walk' when held in a certain way. This body was more cuddly, less likely to break, and once again there was a spate of imitations from many doll companies eager to take part in a lucrative trade.

Walküre 1902–27

*Walküre
Germany*

A registered trademark for a ball jointed composition doll by Kley & Hahn, with heads possibly made by Kestner. Often dolls bearing this trademark can be found dressed in ethnic costume.

Walther & Sohn, mark WS 220 13/0

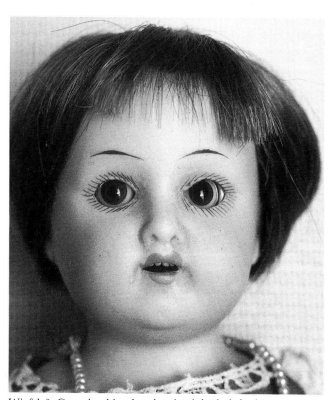

Wiefel & Co., shoulderplate head, pink cloth body

Walther & Sohn (Walther & Son) Oeslau 1908-41, porcelain factory

1908 Porcelain factory was founded by Johann Walther (doll factory owner) and Nikolaus Oberender (porcelain factory).

1910 Walther and Oberender separated and each had his own porcelain factory making dolls' heads.

1910 Walther was exporting bisque dolls' heads to England and America, and by the number of dolls found in this country with the W&S mark, also Australia. The company was closed, but was refounded under new names.

1921 J. Walther & Sohn was the new name of the firm.

1928 Bisque doll heads were featured in their advertising.

1930 Producing bisque doll heads, baby heads and bathing dolls.

1941 Still making bathing dolls, doll heads and baby heads. Until recently the trademark of Walther & Sohn had been incorrectly attributed to Strobel & Wilken.

Walterhausen Puppenfabrik Walterhausen 1902-30 +
After the death of Heinrich Handwerck, his factory was called Walterhausen Puppenfabrik. It was a subsidiary of Kammer & Reinhardt, and became part of the Bing conglomerate in 1924.

Wegner, Herman Sonneberg, Germany, doll factory
1893 Took out a patent for a multi-headed doll, a jointed doll with exchangeable heads.

1908 Patent for a remountable jointed doll with a voice device.

1922 Manufactured baby dolls, jointed dolls and Character dolls of best quality, dressed and undressed.

Welsch & Co. Sonneberg, 1911-25 +, doll factory
1911 Founded by Ferdinand Welsch and Otto Mulhauser.

1917 Became part of the Bing concern, but retained name and remained an independent factory.

1920 Only distributed their dolls through Bing.

From 1911 to 1917 the bisque heads used by the firm were bought mostly from Max Oscar Arnold, hence the MOA Welsch trademarks found on many dolls' heads. After 1917 dolls' heads manufactured by Schutzmeister & Quendt and Simon & Halbig were used on their dolls.

Wiefel & Co. see also Erste Steinbacher Porzellanfabrik. Steinbach, Germany, porcelain factory
The Erste Steinbacher Porzellanfabrik (First Steinbach Porcelain Factory) made dolls' heads using the EStP marking.

1900 Founded by Max Kiesewetter.

Hugo Wiegand, mark H.W./S. *Betty Brown collection*

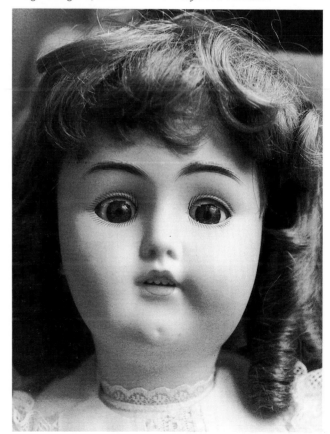

Doll by Adolf Wislizenus, Walterhausen, for B. Illfelder, New York, mark My Sweetheart. *Pearl Porter collection*

1912 Hugo Wiefel took over and began making dolls' heads.

W& Co
Germany

1926 Wiefel retired and his successors were Robert Carl (of Porzellanfabrik Mengersgereuth) and Gustav Heubach.

Wiegand, Hugo Walterhausen, Germany 1911–28 + , doll factory

Germany
H.W.

1911 The firm was founded and registration made for two baby dolls.
1913 Bent limb babies and toddlers were advertised.
1923–26 Took out many patents for various doll movements.
1926 Ma-ma dolls, baby dolls, fully dressed or wearing a chemise, able to sit or stand, were among those advertised.

Wislizenus, Adolf Walterhausen, Germany, doll factory

Heubach Koppelsdorf
A.W.
W
Germany

101
A.W.
MY SWEETHEART
B.J & C₀

A W
Special
Germany

1851 Founded to make papier mâché dolls, Gottlob Schafft the owner.
1870 Adolf Wislizenus took over the factory.
Wislizenus brought Jumeau's ball jointed doll body to Walterhausen.
1878 Adolf Wislizenus sole owner, and he registered three jointed dolls.
1887–96 Continued to work on perfecting doll bodies.
1902 The firm was using Simon & Halbig mould number 1249 for their Old Glory jointed dolls.
1903 Patented a mould to manufacture pressed doll parts.
1911 Character baby dolls with painted or glass eyes were advertised.
1912–29 Specialised in extraordinary ball jointed bodies.
1921 Used a four leaf clover and the initials A.W. over W. as trademark.
1925 Applied for a patent for walking dolls.
1931. Firm went into bankruptcy, and was then acquired by Koenig & Wernicke.
During the years of making dolls, the firm bought bisque dolls' heads from Bahr & Proschild and Simon and Halbig, and after 1910 from Ernst Heubach.

Wolf, Louis New York, USA and Sonneberg, Germany, import house
1900 Sonneberg branch opened.
1904 Displayed dolls at St Louis Exposition and advertised C.M. Bergmann dolls. .
1907–08 Mentioned a factory in Sonneberg and advertised Bergmann dolls.

198/DEP/L.W.&Co/121/A.M./5. *Courtesy Doll & Toy Collection, Brisbane*

L.W.C./2. *Private collection, Queensland*

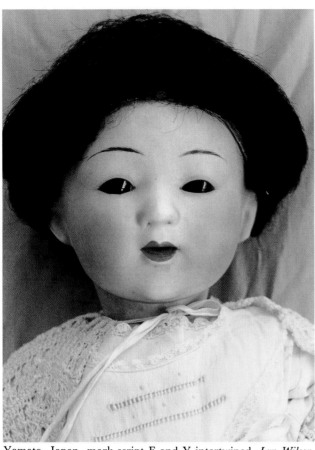

Yamato, Japan, mark script F and Y intertwined. *Lyn Wilson collection*

Script F&Y entwined, Yamato-Japan

1910 Advertised E.U. Steiner's walking doll.
1915 At the Chicago Toy Exhibit showed over 700 styles of foreign Character dolls. Also had a Japanese department with bisque babies made in Japan.

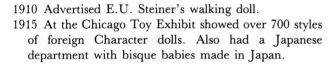

152
L W & C

1916 L.W. & Co. (bisque head mould 152) were advertised.
1919 Japanese manufactured bisque dolls modelled after German designs were advertised.

Yamato Japan 1917–20 + , import/export company
Manufactured bisque dolls and dolls' heads in Japan, which were exported to North America, Ceylon (Sri Lanka) and Australia.
They advertised in America that they were the only genuine bisque dolls made in Japan. This seems an unlikely claim, or was it that they had sculptors to model their own bisque heads, instead of copying German heads. To back this up, there is a lovely Japanese style bisque headed baby doll with Yamato markings in my family.

Unusual body found on dolls by Herman Wegner

Bibliography

Bach, Jean *Collecting German Dolls* Main Street Press,
Secaucus, New Jersey 1983

Borger, Mona *'Chinas': Dolls for Study and Admiration* Borger
Publications, San Francisco, California 1983

Cieslik, Jurgen and Marianne Cieslik *German Doll Encyclopedia
1800-1939* Hobby House Press, Cumberland, Maryland.
English edition 1985

Cieslik, Jurgen and Marianne Cieslik *German Doll Marks and
Identification Book* Hobby House Press, Cumberland,
Maryland 1986

Coleman, Dorothy S, Elizabeth A. Coleman and Evelyn J.
Coleman *The Collector's Encyclopaedia of Dolls* Crown
Publishers, New York 1968

Coleman, Dorothy S., Elizabeth A. Coleman and Evelyn J.
Coleman, *The Collector's Encyclopedia of Dolls* Volume II,
Crown Publishers, New York 1986

Coleman, Elizabeth A. *Dolls: Makers and Marks* 2nd edition,
Washington D.C. 1966

Collier, Julie *The Official Identification and Price Guide to Antique
and Modern Dolls* House of Collectables, New York 1989

Darbyshire, Lydia (editor) *The Collector's Encyclopedia of Toys
and Dolls* New Burlington Books, London 1990

Fainges, Marjory *Australian Dollmakers—A History* Kangaroo
Press 1986

Fawdry, Kenneth and Marguerite Fawdry *Pollock's History of
English Dolls and Toys* Ernest Benn, London 1979

Foulke, Jan *Kestner, King of Dollmakers* Hobby House Press,
Cumberland, Maryland 1982

Foulkeu, Jan *8th Blue Book Dolls and Values* Hobby House
Press, Cumberland, Maryland 1987

Foulke, Jan *9th Blue Book Dolls and Values* Hobby House
Press, Cumberland, Maryland

Frame, Linda *Folk and Foreign Costume Dolls* Collector Books,
Kentucky 1980

Goodfellow, Caroline C. *Understanding Dolls* Antique
Collectors Club, Baron Publishers, Woodbridge, England
1983

Hillier, Mary *Automata and Mechanical Toys* Jupiter Books,
London 1976

Hillier, Mary (editor) *Pollock's Dictionary of English Dolls*
Robert Hale Ltd, London 1982

Hillier, Mary *The History of Wax Dolls* Souvenir Press,
London 1985

Holz, Loretta *The How-to Book of International Dolls* Crown
Publishers, New York 1980

King, Constance Eileen *The Price Guide to Dolls Antique and
Modern* Antique Collectors Club, Woodbridge, Suffollk
1977

King, Constance Eileen *Jumeau, Prince of Dollmakers* New
Cavendish Books, London 1983

Lavitt, Wendy *Dolls* The Knopf Collectors' Guides to
American Antiques, Alfred A. Knopf, New York 1983

Mansell, Colette *The Collector's Guide to British Dolls Since 1920*
Robert Hale, London 1983

Marion, Frieda *China Half Figures called Pincushion Dolls*
Collector Books, Kentucky 1974

Merrill, Madeline Obsorne *The Art of Dolls 1700-1940*
Robert Hale, London 1985

Porot, Anne Marie, Jacques Theimer and François Theimer
S.F.B.J. Captivating Character Children Hobby House Press,
Cumberland, Maryland 1986

Richter, Lydia *Treasury of French Dolls* Album 2, H.P. Books,
Tuscon, English publication 1984

Smith, Patricia R. *Modern Collector's Dolls* First Edition
Collectors' Books, Kentucky 1973

Smith, Patricia R. *China and Parian Dolls, Featuring Stone
Bisque and Tinted Bisque* Collector Books, Kentucky 1980

Whitton, Margaret *The Jumeau Doll* Dover Publications Inc.,
New York 1980.

Magazines
Australian Doll Digest Goulburn, NSW
Doll Reader Hobby House Press, Maryland, USA

Index

MOULD NUMBERS